THE JEWS OF ENGLAND

5-2-89

This book is dedicated to Jamie (still).

Second Edition 1988
First published as *Anglo-Jewry In Evidence* in 1985 by
The Michael Goulston Educational Foundation,
The Sternberg Centre for Judaism
80 East End Road, London, N.3.
in association with Jewish Chronicle Publications Ltd
Copyright © 1985 Jonathan A. Romain
ISBN 0 907372 04
Typeset by Edgewood Stationers Ltd.
Production in association with
Book Production Consultants, Cambridge.
Printed in Great Britain by St. Edmundsbury Press,
Bury St. Edmunds, Suffolk.

THE JEWS OF ENGLAND

A Portrait of Anglo-Jewry through Original Sources and Illustrations

Jonathan A. Romain

with contributions by Jon Epstein & Amanda Golby

Jonathan A. Romain

Born in 1954, Jonathan Romain graduated from University College, London in Jewish History and Hebrew Literature, and then studied for the Rabbinate at the Leo Baeck College. Since 1980, he has been the Rabbi of the Maidenhead Synagogue, and is also engaged in post-graduate studies in Anglo-Jewry. His previous publications for the Goulston Foundation are ''Signs and Wonders — A New Method of Teaching Beginners' Hebrew'' and (with Bernard Kops) ''In A Strange Land—A History of the Jews in Modern Times''. He is married with two sons.

Jon Epstein

Jon Epstein was born in 1944. He read Geography at Cambridge and is now head of Upper School at Tiffins School, Kingston-upon-Thames. He has taught Anglo-Jewish History in Religion Schools for several years, and has also helped produce local history packs in Kingston. He is currently Chairman of the North Western Reform Synagogue, London.

Amanda Golby

Born in 1953, Amanda Golby has a law degree and a diploma in librarianship. She has worked in several libraries, including University of London and City of London Polytechnic. She has also worked as indexer to ''The Jewish Chronicle''. She was ordained as a Rabbi at the Leo Baeck College in 1988 and is minister of Southport Reform Synagogue.

The Michael Goulston Educational Foundation

The Michael Goulston Educational Foundation was established in 1972 to continue the pioneering educational work of the late Rabbi Michael Goulston. It produces material for teaching all aspects of the Jewish Heritage that relate to the contemporary world, using modern educational concepts and multi-media techniques.

Contents

Preface

There are many histories of Anglo-Jewry, the most notable being that by Cecil Roth. However, few provide original sources or contemporary illustrations for the events that they describe. *The Jews of England* is designed to fill this gap. Its purpose is to offer both the student of history and the interested reader material with which to make their own investigations and to form their own judgements. Naturally, considerations of space have set a limit to the range of subjects and the depth in which they have been explored. However, the material included is sufficient to give a broad impression of the social and political history of Anglo-Jewry. Those wishing to pursue certain areas further will be assisted by the 'Background Reading' lists suggested at the end of each chapter and the 'Further Reading' list recommended at the end of the book.

The Jews of England is also intended for use in Religion Schools, Adult Education Classes, further education colleges and secondary schools that are covering all or parts of Anglo-Jewish history. A Teachers' Guide giving further information, suggesting discussion topics and providing follow-up activities is available from the Michael Goulston Educational Foundation.

Two chapters in particular may require a brief word of explanation. Although not specifically an Anglo-Jewish phenomenon, Zionism (Chapter 25) has certainly been an active force in Anglo-Jewry. Moreover, the fact that Palestine was administered by the British authorities makes the subject particularly relevant to a history of Anglo-Jewry. The final chapter (*Recent Decades*) is perhaps the most controversial. It is difficult to know what events of one's own time will seem important in later years, but I felt it was right to try to chronicle the most recent developments within Anglo-Jewry in this text. In a few years' time, hindsight will indicate whether the selection was appropriate or not.

Finally, some credits to those who assisted with this publication — especially to Jon Epstein and Amanda Golby who made many suggestions and contributions and carefully scrutinised the text in manuscript form. Trudy Gold, Irene Kay, Jackie Martin, Audrey Mindlin and Jennifer Sampson each gave valuable help at various stages. Thanks are also due to Rabbi Tony Bayfield, Rabbi Michael Heilbron and Margaret Sassienie of the R.S.G.B. Education Department for their encouragement throughout the project.

Jonathan A. Romain
March 1985

It has been the good fortune of the first edition to have been sold out and also to have been greeted with favourable reviews. This, the second edition, has provided the opportunity to add two more chapters and several new illustrations. Another thank you is necessary—to David Pelham for assisting so helpfully with all the arrangements. The facilities provided by the Mocatta Library are also appreciated.

J.A.R.
May 1988

Note
B.C.E. indicates Before the Common Era (or B.C.)
C.E. indicates Common Era (or A.D.)

Introduction

Compared to other Jewish communities in Europe, the Jews of England are recent arrivals. In 1066 French, German and Italian Jewry had been established for almost a millennium, whereas Anglo-Jewry was only just coming into existence. The Norman Conquest marked the beginnings of the community, but it did not settle long. In the 13th century, the Jews of England were expelled and it was not until the time of Cromwell, 400 years later, that Anglo-Jewry was re-established. On both occasions the arrival of the Jews is hard to pinpoint exactly, but the entry of a few individuals quickly led to the formation of a small and expanding community. Both settlements started in London, and then spread throughout the country, although London Jewry always remained the largest and most influential of the communities.

The history of mediaeval Anglo-Jewry largely reflects that of Jews throughout the mediaeval world. Initially, life was relatively peaceful and prosperous, and Jews and Christians often had friendly relations with one another. However, Jews were soon condemned by Christian society to the role of moneylenders, and their position began to deteriorate rapidly. They were also taxed at a punishingly high rate, forced to wear distinctive clothing by an increasingly hostile Church, and subject to blood libels, riots and conversionist activities. Eventually, when they were no longer profitable for the king, the Jews were expelled. In fact, England has the dubious honour of being the first country to have a blood libel and to order a mass expulsion of its Jews, and both of these practices were quickly imitated in other parts of Europe.

The Jews who were re-admitted in the 17th century, found themselves with a mixed legacy. In the popular mind they were identified with Shakespeare's money-grabbing Shylock or Marlowe's poisonous Barabas; to Cromwell, however, they were industrious merchants and financiers with international connections, who could be of great service to the New Commonwealth. In practice this pragmatic attitude prevailed, and the tolerant welcome extended to the Jews was continued by Charles II and his successors. Unlike Jewry elsewhere in Europe, largely oppressed and denied any social or economic opportunities until the French Revolution, Anglo-Jewry suffered few disabilities and had access to all levels of society. Although the political emancipation of Anglo-Jewry came comparatively late in 1858, this was partly because Anglo-Jewry enjoyed so many other privileges it had not regarded political equality as so essential.

In the 20th century, the two major events affecting world Jewry — the Holocaust and the State of Israel — made their impact on Anglo-Jewry too. The rise of Nazi Germany was responsible for a wave of immigrants from Central Europe. They considerably bolstered the numbers and talents of Anglo-Jewry, as had the influx of East European Jews two generations earlier. The struggle for a Jewish homeland and the birth of the State of Israel initially led to some friction with the government during the British administration of Palestine. However, fears that English Jews would be suspected of harbouring 'dual loyalty' have not materialised. Since 1948, Israel has not only offered an opportunity for English Jews to make aliyah[1], but has also given those who are happy to remain in England an added sense of pride and has strengthened their Jewish identity.

During the Middle Ages, continental Jews would mourn for the Jews of England, reciting every Tishah be-Av[2] an elegy for those killed in the York Massacre of 1190. Nowadays Anglo-Jewry is regarded as one of the success stories of modern Jewish history. Long may it remain so.

1. *Immigration to the Land of Israel.*
2. *Fast commemorating the destruction of the Temple and other tragic events in Jewish history.*

Fig 1. A mediaeval Jew, with a Jewish hat, pointed and coloured green.

1

The First Records

It is quite likely that individual Jews visited and even lived in England as early as Roman times. However, there was no settled community until 1066, when Jews from Normandy came to England in the footsteps of William the Conqueror. Anglo-Jewry was thus an extension of French Jewry and very similar in its lifestyle and general culture. Initially the Jews resided in London, but gradually they spread elsewhere, particularly to the larger towns, where royal protection would be more effective than in outlying areas. Only a few records of the early years remain:

1.1   **1075 Jews settle in Oxford**

About this time I find the Jews settled and their number great in Oxford, as in several scripts[1] it appears, particularly in that of Brumman le Riche, made to the said church of St. George at its first foundation, by which giving to the canons thereof land in Walton, in the north suburbs of Oxford, warranteth it to them "against Jews."[2]

Anthony à Wood

1. *Letters*
2. *A guarantee that the rights of the land would not be transferred to Jews (which could lead to the crown claiming the land as the Jews themselves were regarded as the property of the crown).*

1.2   **1086 A Jewish Name in the Domesday Book**

Alwi sheriff holds from the king two hides[3] and a half at Blicestone (Oxfordshire).

This land Manasses[4] bought from him without license of the king[5].

The same bishop holds Staplebridge (Dorset). Of the same

land Manasses holds three virgates[6] which William, the king's son, took from the church without the consent of the bishops and monks.

Domesday Book

3. *A measure of land, approximately 120 acres.*
4. *A corruption of 'Manasseh'.*
5. *Necessary for land transactions, marriages, custody of children and other legal matters engaged in by Jews.*
6. *A measure of land, approximately 30 acres.*

1.3 c.1090 William II Jokes With The Jews

The Jews who dwelt in London, whom his (Rufus') father had brought thither from Rouen, approached on a certain solemn occasion, bringing him gifts; he bent down to them and even dared to animate them to a conflict[7] against the Christians. 'By the face of Luke', quoth he, declaring that if they conquered he would join their sect.

William of Malmesbury *Gesta Rerum Anglicanarum*

7. *A debate*

Background Reading:
Cecil Roth *A History of the Jews in England p.1-5.*

Figure 2. Mosse-Mokke of Norwich 1233, wearing the spiked hat prescribed for Jews as a mark of identity by the 1215 Lateran Council.

2

Everyday Life in the Middle Ages

The early years of Jewish settlement in England were marked by generally good relations between Jews and non-Jews. While the Jews had their own religious and cultural institutions, and mixed largely amongst themselves, they also had considerable social and economic contacts with non-Jews, which included debating with clerics, being involved in monastic politics, drinking with gentile neighbours, and using their medical skills and charms. Jews would often live together in the same street or quarter, but there were no ghettos[1], and Jews and non-Jews would visit each other's houses.

1. *Areas to which Jewish residence was limited.*

2.1   Before 1096 Friendly Debate Between Christian and Jew.

To the Rev. Father and Lord Anselm, Archbishop of the holy Church of Canterbury, his servant and son, Brother Gilbert (Crispin), proctor and servant of Westminster Abbey, wisheth prosperous continuance in this life and a blissful eternity in the future one.

I send you a little work to be submitted to your fatherly prudence. I wrote it recently, putting to paper what a Jew said when formerly disputing with me against our faith in defence of his own law, and what I replied in favour of the faith against his objections. I know not where he was born, but he was educated at Mayence; he was well versed even in our law and literature, and had a mind practised in the Scriptures and in disputes against us. He often used to come to me as a friend both for business and to see me, since in certain things I was very necessary to him, and as often as we came together we would soon get talking in a friendly spirit about the Scriptures and our faith. Now on a certain day God granted both him and me greater leisure than usual, and soon we began questioning as usual. And as his objections were consequent and logical, and as he explained with equal consequence his former objections, while our reply met his objections foot to foot, and by his own confession seemed equally supported by the testimony of the Scriptures, some of the bystanders requested me to preserve our disputes as likely to be of use to others in future.

St. Anselm *Opera*

2.2   1182 Jews of Bury St. Edmunds in a Monastic Controversy

But William, the Sacristan, had a suspicion of his associate, Samson, and so had many others who favoured the side of the said William, both Christians and Jews. Jews, I say, for to them the Sacristan was said to be a father and a patron. They used to enjoy his protection, and had free entrance and exit, and often went through the monastery, wandering through the altars and around the shrine while the solemnities of the Mass were being celebrated. And their moneys were placed in our treasury in the charge of the sacristan, and, what was more absurd, their wives and little ones were received in our refectory in time of war.

Jocelin de Brakeland *Chronica*

Fig. 3. Moyse's Hall, Bury St. Edmunds, Suffolk, believed to have been a synagogue before the expulsion of the Jewish community from the town in 1190 by the Abbot Samson. He had triumphed over his rival, William the Sacristan, whom the Jews had supported.

2.3   Before 1184 Jews drink with non-Jews

It is surprising that in the land of the Isle (England) they are lenient in the matter of drinking strong drinks of the Gentiles and along with them. For the Law is distinctly according to those Doctors[2] who forbid it on the ground that it leads to intermarriage. But perhaps, as there would be great ill-feeling if they were to refrain from this, one must not be severe upon them.

Elhanan ben Isaac Tosaphot

2.   Rabbis

2.4   Before 1193 The result of entering a Jewish House

By a similar piety we know Godeliva of Canterbury to have been seized, who taking some water (sanctified by St. Thomas) in a wooden bucket, was passing through the inn of a certain Jew and entered it at the invitation of a Jewish woman. For being skilled in charms and incantations she was accustomed to charm the weak foot of the Jewess. But scarcely had her foot entered the abominate house when the bucket flew into three pieces and by the loss of the water she learned the wicked intuitions of her own mind, and understanding that she had committed a fault she returned no more to that Jewess.

J. C. Robertson Materials for History of Thomas Beckett

Much of Jewish life was governed by the decisions of the Rabbis, some of whom were well-known abroad for their learning:

2.5   c.1171 A Rabbinic Decision

The question is whether you may buy milk from a Gentile drawn from the animal without any Jew being present[3]. Rabbi Benjamin of Canterbury forbids it, even in the case where the Gentile has no unclean animal among his flocks.

Mordecai ben Hillel Sefer Mordecai

3.   Normally a Jew would be present to ensure that the milk does not come into contact with the produce of an animal that is defined as unclean by the Bible (i.e. which is not cloven-hoofed or does not chew the cud — see Leviticus Chapter 11).

Fig. 4. Jew weighing coins to guard against coin-clipping 1233. Coin-clipping — removing the precious metals for other uses — was a common crime in the Middle Ages and an accusation often levelled against the Jews.

2.6   Before 1200 Decision of Rabbi Menachem of London

The case came before Rabbi Perez concerning a divorce given by one whose name had been changed when he was thought to be *in articulo mortis*, and they called him by the new first name henceforth[4]. The Rabbi decided that two bills of divorce should be written, one with the old first name and the other with the new, and the two were to be given to the woman simultaneously[5]. I found it written in an exposition (Midrash) of Rabbi Menachem of London that it is necessary to write the two names, for we find it with Jacob, of whom it is written in the Law[6]: "And thy name shall no more be called Jacob but

17

Israel," and yet one finds him called Jacob several times in the Law.

Judah ben Eliezer *Minhat Yehuda*

4. So that the Angel of Death, looking for the 'old' person, will be confused, and not take the life of the 'new' person.
5. So that there be no doubt about the divorce's validity.
6. Genesis Chapter 32, Verse 29.

Other records relating to everyday life are:

2.7   1177 Jewish Cemeteries

The same year the lord the king gave a licence to the Jews of his land to have a cemetery in any city of England beyond the walls of the cities, where they might buy a place for burying their dead reasonably and in a suitable spot: for previously all dead Jews used to be carried to London to be buried[7].

Roger de Hovedene *Chronica*

7. In Cripplegate. Cemeteries were later established in Bristol, Cambridge, Canterbury, Northampton, Norwich, Oxford and York.

2.8   1181 Jews Forbidden To Carry Arms

Also no Jew shall keep with him mail or hauberk[8], but let him sell or give them away, or in some other way remove them from him so that they may remain in the service of the king of England[9].

Roger de Hovedene *Chronica*

8. A military tunic.
9. Jews did not usually serve in the army as they were outside the feudal framework.

2.9   1199 King John Appoints An Adviser

The King to all his subjects and to all both Jews and English greeting. Know that we have granted and by this present charter of ours have confirmed to Jacob, Jew of London, priest of the Jews, the presbyterate[10] of all the Jews of the whole of England, to have and to hold as long as he lives freely and quietly, honourably and fully, so that no one thereon shall presume to offer him any hurt or hindrance. Wherefore we will and firmly order that you shall guarantee and maintain and guard in peace the presbyterate of all the Jews throughout England to the same Jacob so long as he lives.

Charter Rolls

10. *The King's expert on Jewish affairs.*

Fig. 5. Abigail, wife of Mosse-Mokke of Norwich 1233. She is wearing the fashionable coif and wimple of the period.

2.10   1249 A Marriage Agreement

The contract between Yomtov ben Moses and Solomon ben Eliab, and these are the conditions which they agreed upon when the aforesaid Yomtov betrothed his daughter Zeuna to the aforesaid Solomon, and he agreed to give him a dowry of 10 marks at the time of the wedding and a further 5 marks a year later. He will also provide the bridegroom and the bride with weekday and Sabbath clothing, and give them full board and lodging. And the aforesaid Yomtov undertakes to sustain and support the bridegroom and the bride a full year in his home and supply them with all necessities and to clothe and shoe them, and to pay their taxes if any are imposed on them during that year. He will also hire a teacher[9] for the duration of that year. The wedding will be, God willing, in the month of Nisan[10] 1249, providing no obstacle arises. If, God forbid, some obstacle arises, then the wedding will be held one month after it has passed ... And if, God forbid, one of the parties breaks off this agreement, then he shall pay the other 5 marks.

Norwich Betrothal Contract

9. *For the bridegroom.*
10. *A Hebrew month, falling in March-April.*

Fig. 6. Isaac of Norwich 1288 ('Hake' is a diminutive form of 'Isaac').

2.11 Early 13th Century Jewish Code of Education

The teachers shall not take more than ten students in one subject. For though our Sages have fixed 25 as the proper number of students for one teacher, that applied only to

Palestine where the climate favoured the development of the mind, and for the time of political independence, for in freedom the mind is lofty, strong, clear and light, and takes up wisdom and knowledge easier than in a state of subjection.

*

The teacher shall not teach the boys by heart but from the book, and teach them to translate the Bible into the vernacular. The Sages used to go through the weekly readings on Sabbath twice in the original and once in translation, twice in the original for we always read anything we love twice over, and once in translation to make God's word understanded of the women and the vulgar[11] so that perchance the fear of God might enter their hearts.

*

The teachers shall accustom the lads to examine one another every evening in their lessons, so that they may sharpen one another's wits.

*

The teachers should make the lads repeat every Friday what they have learnt in the current and in the preceding week.

*

During the winter nights ... each lad shall pay something for the lights.

*

How shall the boys be educated and the tasks be set by the teachers?

Our sages say (Avot 5.24)[12] at five years to the Scriptures. At that age a father shall hand him over to a teacher at the beginning of the month Nisan. The father shall expressly

21

determine the teacher's work, saying to him, "Know that you shall teach my son the alphabet this month, the vowels next month, and how to put them together in syllables in the third. Thenceforward shall 'the pure deal with the pure', i.e., with Leviticus.[13]

From month to month you shall increase my son's task. If this month he can learn half the weekly portion of Scripture, next month he must go through the whole. From Tammuz to Tishri[14] he must go through the weekly portion in Hebrew, and from Tishri to Nisan in the vernacular. Then the boy is six years old. In his seventh year he must learn the Aramaic version from the book and not by heart and translate it into the vulgar tongue. In his eighth and ninth year he must take the prophets and Hagiographa."

Our sages say further: At ten years to the Mishnah. ... for all this a space of 3 years is appointed, for then the lad is 13 years old.

Gudemann *Geschichte*

11.   *The uneducated.*
12.   *Tractate of the Mishnah, the Rabbinic commentary on the Hebrew Bible.*
13.   *The Biblical book containing the laws of ritual purity.*
14.   *Hebrew months, approximately covering June to September.*

Fig. 7. Isaac fil Jurnet of Norwich 1233. One of the wealthiest Jews of his day (hence the coronet). He is facing three ways to allude to the extent of his financial dealings.

Background Reading:
Cecil Roth *A Day in the Life of a Mediaeval Jew* in *Essays and Portraits in Anglo-Jewish History* p.26-45.
Dietary Laws in *Encyclopaedia Judaica* Vol.6 Col.26-45.
Israel Abrahams *Jewish Life in the Middle Ages.*

Fig. 7a. Caricature of Norwich Jews.

3

Charter to the Jews

As newcomers to England, the Jews had no established rights or place in the feudal hierarchy. They were made directly responsible to the king, and royal charters confirmed their position. The charter of Henry I, now lost, was the model for all subsequent ones.

3.1   1201 Confirmation of the Charters of the Jews

Charter of the Jews of England. — John, by the grace of God, &c. I. — Know that we have granted to all the Jews of England and Normandy to have freely and honourably residence in our land, and to hold all that from us which they held from King Henry, our father's grandfather, and all that now they reasonably hold in land and fees and mortgages and goods, and that they have all their liberties and customs just as they had them in the time of the aforesaid King Henry, our father's grandfather, better and more quietly and more honourably.

II. — And if any dispute arise between a Christian and a Jew he who summons the other to answer his complaint should have witnesses, viz.: a lawful Christian and a lawful Jew. And if a Jew has a writ about his complaint the writ shall be a witness for him, and if a Christian have a complaint against a Jew let it be judged by peers of the Jew.

III. — And when a Jew dies his body shall not be detained above earth, but his heirs shall have his money and his debts, so that he shall not be disturbed therefore if he has an heir who may answer for him and do what is right about his debts and his forfeit. And let it be lawful for Jews to receive and buy without difficulty all things that may be brought to them except things of the church[1] or blood-stained cloth.[2]

IV. — And if any Jew is summoned by anyone without

testimony, he shall be quits of that summons on his sole oath on his Book.[3] And on the summons of those things that belong to our crown he shall be quits on his sole oath on his roll. And if there is a dispute between Christian and Jew about accommodation of some money the Jew shall prove the capital and the Christian the interest.

V. — And let it be lawful to the Jew to sell his pledge after it is certain that he has held it for a whole year and one day. And Jews shall not enter into pleadings except before us and before those who guard our castles in whose bailiwicks the Jews dwell.[4]

VI. — And wherever the Jews may be let it be lawful for them to go when they will with all their chattels just as our own property[5], and let none stop or prevent them in this.

VII. — And we order that they be free through all England and Normandy of all the customs and tolls and modiation of wine just as our own chattels.[5] And we order you to guard, to defend, and to maintain them. And we prohibit anyone from summoning them against their charter on the above points on our forfeit[6] such as the charter of King Henry our father reasonably declares. Witnesses Godfrey son of Peter Earl of Essex, &c. Given at Marlborough the tenth day of April in the second year of our reign.

Charter Rolls

1. *For the sake of the honour of the Church.*
2. *To avoid possible accusations of a blood libel (see Chapter 4).*
3. *The Hebrew Bible.*
4. *Thus avoiding the (often hostile) ordinary or church courts.*
5. *The legal position of the Jews.*
6. *To our injury.*

All transactions were written in Hebrew and Latin on a starr (from 'shetar' — Hebrew for a legal document) and kept in special chests (archae) in the charge of local royal officials.

Fig. 8. A starr c.1236

Background Reading:

Cecil Roth *A History of the Jews in England* p.6 (also: archae p.29; starr p.110-111).

H. G. Richardson *English Jewry under Angevin Kings* p.109-110.

4

The Blood Libel

The "Blood Libel" was one of the greatest lies perpetrated against the Jews, and originated in England with the case of William of Norwich in 1144. According to the libel, Jews showed their hatred of Christianity by re-enacting the Crucifixion and murdering a Christian child at Easter time. A later development of the libel suggested that the Jews used the child's blood to make unleavened bread for Passover, a Jewish festival which usually occurs at the same time as Easter. Despite being condemned by several mediaeval Popes, the "Blood Libel" spread throughout Europe, where it persisted into the early 20th century.

4.1   1144 William of Norwich

Now will we say something of what befel in king Stephen's time. In his time the Jews of Norwich bought a Christian child before Easter and tortured him with all the tortures wherewith our Lord was tortured, and on Long Friday hanged him on a rood in hatred of our Lord, and afterwards buried him.[1] They thought it would be concealed, but our Lord showed that he was a holy martyr. And the monks took him and buried him honourably in the monastery, and through our Lord he makes wonderful and manifold miracles, and he is hight Saint William.[2]

Old English Chronicles

1.   *In fact, the sheriff regarded the evidence against the Jews as too scanty to justify a trial. Long Friday is a Saxon name for Good Friday, the Friday preceding Easter Day. A rood is a cross.*
2.   *A shrine brought considerable prestige and benefit to local clergy,*

Another Blood Libel was immortalised in the Prioress's Tale in Chaucer's *The Canterbury Tales* (written 1386):

27

In Asia once there was a christian town
In which, long since, a Ghetto³ used to be
Where there were Jews, supported by the Crown
For the foul lucre of their usury,
Hateful to Christ and all his company.
And through this Ghetto one might walk or ride
For it was free and open, either side.

Among these children was a widow's son,
A little chorister of seven years old,
And day by day to school he used to run
And had the custom (for he had been told
To do so) should he happen to behold
An image of Christ's mother, to kneel and say
Hail Mary as he went upon his way.

As I have said, this child would go along
The Jewish street and, of his own accord,
Daily and merrily he sang his song
O Alma Redemptoris; as it soared,
The sweetness of the mother of our Lord
Would pierce his heart, he could not choose but pray
And sing as, to and fro, he went his way.

First of our foes, the Serpent Satan shook
Those Jewish hearts that are his waspish nest,
Swelled up and said, 'O Hebrew people, look!
Is this not something that should be redressed?
Is such a boy to roam as he thinks best
Singing, to spite you, canticles and saws
Against the reverence of your holy laws?'

From that time forward all these Jews conspired
To chase this innocent child from the earth's face.
Down a dark alley-way they found and hired
A murderer who owned that secret place;
And as the boy passed at his happy pace
This cursed Jew grabbed him and held him, slit

His little throat and cast him in a pit.

Cast him, I say, into a privy-drain,
Where they were wont to void their excrement.
O cursed folk! O Herod come again[4],
What profit was there in your foul intent?
Murder will out, and nothing can prevent
God's honour spreading, even from such seed;
The blood cries out upon your cursed deed.

This wretched widow waited all that night,
She waited for her child, but all for nought;
And so, soon as there came the morning light
Pale on her face of dread and busy thought,
She searched his school, then up and down she sought
Elsewhere, and finally she got the news
That he was last seen in the street of Jews.

She made enquiry with a piteous cry
Of every Jew inhabiting that place,
Asking if they had seen her child go by,
And they said, 'No'. But Jesus of His grace
Put in her thought, after a little space,
To come upon that alley as she cried
Where, in a pit, he had been cast aside.

The Provost then did judgement on the men
Who did the murder, and he bid them serve
A shameful death in torment there and then
On all those guilty Jews; he did not swerve.
'Evils shall meet the evils they deserve.'
And he condemned them to be drawn apart
By horses. Then he hanged them from a cart.

O Hugh of Lincoln, likewise murdered so[5]
By cursed Jews, as is notorious
(For it was but a little time ago),
Pray mercy on our faltering steps, that thus
Merciful God reach mercy down to us,
Though we be so unstable, though we vary,
In love and reverence of His mother Mary.

Amen.

3. Ghettos (enclosed areas in a town, to which Jewish residence was limited) did not exist in England, although there were voluntary Jewish quarters.
4. Referring to Herod's supposed 'massacre of the innocents' (Matthew Chapter 32, verse 16) now known to have no historical basis.
5. It is more likely that Hugh accidentally fell into the cesspool whilst at play. As a result of the libel 19 Jews were hanged and 80 others imprisoned.

Fig. 9.
"Martyrdom of William of Norwich"

Hugh of Lincoln was buried in a splendid shrine in the Cathedral, which became a centre for pilgrimages. The shrine remained there until 1928, when it was replaced by a plaque:

4.3   1928 A Retraction

Trumped-up stories of ritual murder of Christian boys by Jewish communities were common throughout Europe during the Middle Ages and even much later. These fictions cost many innocents their lives. Lincoln had its own legend and the alleged victim was buried in the Cathedral in the year 1255. Such stories do not redound to the honour of Christendom, and so we pray:

Remember not, Lord, our offences; nor the offences of our forefathers.

Plaque at Lincoln Cathedral

Background Reading:
Cecil Roth *A History of the Jews in England* p.9, 56-7.
"Blood Libel" in *Encyclopaedia Judaica* Vol. 4 Col. 1120-1131.

St. Hugo's Tomb
as it stands in D.' Stukeley's
Itinerar.

Fig. 9a. The original tomb of Little St. Hugh of Lincoln. Lincoln Cathedral.

5

Aaron of Lincoln

Moneylending — or usury — was a common activity amongst Jews in mediaeval England. This was not from choice, however, but out of necessity, as many other occupations were barred to Jews: to be an artisan generally meant belonging to one of the guilds, all of which were exclusively Christian, while farming involved owning land and hiring Christian labour, both of which were often prohibited to Jews. As Christians were forbidden by Canon Law to be moneylenders, the job was one of the few open to Jews and in constant demand. Moneylending could prove profitable, it was also very risky; when debts remained unpaid, the Jews responsible for collecting them became the focus of resentment and bad feeling.

One of the best-known and wealthiest Jews of mediaeval England was Aaron of Lincoln. His financial operations extended to 25 counties, in 19 of which he maintained his own agents. So great was his personal fortune that, when he died in 1186, Henry II established a special branch of the Exchequer — Scaccarium Aaronis — to deal with his estate, which had been declared the property of the Crown.

5.1   1173 Aaron And The Bishop

Godfrey the son (natural) of king Henry II succeeded him (bishop Chesney 1166) in the rule of Lincoln Minster, the bishopric having fallen into great financial difficulties for many years previously; he was raised to the bishopric of the same see of Lincoln in which he had been archdeacon. And among his very first acts, he immediately redeemed the ornaments of his church[1] which his predecessor had pledged with Aaron the Jew.

Giraldus Cambrensis *Vita S. Remigii*

1. *Pledging Church ornaments was banned by the 1201 Charter — and may already have been by earlier ones (see Chapter 3, Note 1).*

Alexander the Abbot and the Convent of Melsa (Meaux) owe one mark that it may be inscribed on the Great Roll that it has been put on record by the Baron that they have produced a charter of Aaron the Jew of quittance of the debt of William Fossard which charter was released to the said William in presence of the Barons. And these are the words of the charter:

"Know all men reading and hearing these letters that I, Aaron, Jew of Lincoln, by the attestation of this my charter have cried quits to William Fossard of all the debts which he or his father owed unto me; and I testify that he is quit of the debt which he owed either to me or to Josce of York[2] or to the remaining Jews mentioned, viz. Kersun, Elyas, Sanson, Ysaac Jew of Pulcella, or Pulcella herself, or Deulecresse of "Denmark", up to the feast of St. Michael in the year of the incarnation of the Lord, MCLXXVI. This quit claim I have made him for MCCLX marks from which the monks of Melsa have acquitted him towards me. And it is to be known that I have handed over to him certain charters of this debt and if I have any others still in my possession I will hand them over as soon as possible."[3]

Pipe Rolls

2. *Josce of York was one of Aaron of Lincoln's principal agents; he was among the York martyrs who died in 1190.*
3. *This is the first starr on record.*

5.3   **1179 An I.O.U.**

Know, &c., I, Richard of Bisebrok, owe Aaron the Jew of Lincoln ten pounds sterling which I received from him at the octave of St. Michael next after the death of Richard de Luci (ob. 1179) and for each pound I will give him every week two pence for interest as long as I keep the debt by his favour, and for the whole debt aforesaid, viz. capital and interest, I have pledged to him all my land[3] of Bisebrok till he has the debt aforesaid, viz. capital and interest, and if I cannot warrant this land to him I will give him equivalent of its value at his pleasure and this I make affidavit to keep and I, Robert, parson of

Bisebrok, am surety for the whole debt aforesaid, viz. capital
and interest, for satisfying the said Aaron within 15 days of his
summons unless the aforesaid Richard has done it and this is my
affidavit.

The Record Office

*3.   Jews usually sold land that came to them as a result of lost pledges
and thus played a considerable role in the transfer of land from the
lower nobility and gentry to the larger magnates and religious
communities.*

*Fig. 10. 12th century house in Lincoln, traditionally known as Aaron the Jew's House,
although his was a similar building higher up the hill.*

5.4   Before 1183 The Boasting of Aaron of Lincoln

Abbot Simon dying left his Abbey in debt for more than 600 marks to the Jews besides other debts[4] which exceeded the sum of 200 marks and more. Whereupon Aaron the Jew who held us in his debt coming to the House of St. Alban in great pride and boasting, with threats kept on boasting that it was he who had made the window for òur St. Alban, and that he had prepared for the saint a home when without one.[5]

Walsingham *Gesta Abbatium St. Albani*

4.   *To Christians, and therefore not bearing interest, which was banned by Canon Law.*
5.   *Aaron of Lincoln also assisted the building of nine Cistercian abbeys and the cathedrals of Lincoln and Peterborough.*

5.5   1187 Aaron's Treasures Lost At Sea

(The King was detained three days at Dover before he could cross to Witsand, 17th Feb).

But in the meantime a great part of the king's retinue wishing to cross to Normandy were drowned in the sea between Shoreham and Dieppe, with a large part of the treasures[6] of Aaron the Jew of Lincoln, deceased.

Benedict the Abbot *Gesta Henrici*

6.   *The money was being sent to France to assist the war against Philip Augustus. The outstanding credits at the time of Aaron of Lincoln's death amounted to £15,000, equivalent to ¾ of the royal revenue in a normal year.*

Figure 11. Chirograph Recording Sale of Land Adjacent to the Old Jewish Cemetery to the Commune of the Jews of York, c.1230.

The document is half of a sheet, the other half being an exact copy, with the buyer and seller having one each. It is signed in Latin and in Hebrew by Isaac of Northampton, Samuel Cohen, Samuel son of Josce, Josce of Kent, and Josce nephew of Aaron.

Background Reading:

Cecil Roth *A History of the Jews in England* p.15-16.
H. G. Richardson *English Jewry under Angevin Kings* p.115-116.

6

Coronation Riots

The Crusading fervour — which had led to riots against Continental Jewry in the 11th century — spread to England when Richard I succeeded to the throne and pledged to fulfil his father's vow to go on Crusade. The prospect of the Third Crusade, like those before it, set alight anti-Jewish passions.

6.1   1189 The Massacre at Richard I.'s Coronation

Richard, then the only king thus named for a century, was hallowed to king at London and solemnly crowned by Baldwin, archbishop of Canterbury, on Sept 3. There had come together for the solemn anointing of the Christian prince from all quarters of England, not alone Christian nobles, but likewise the chiefs of the Jews. For these enemies of truth fearing that the good luck they had under the former king might be less favourable to them under the new, brought first fruits most decorous and honourable, and hoped to find favour equal to the multitude of their gifts. But he, either because he was less favourable to them than his father, or having some premonition, a certain superstitious foreboding about the plans of certain persons, by an edict, it is said, forbade them entry either into the church where he was being crowned or to the palace where he was banquetting after the coronation. Now it happened that while he was at the repast with all the assembly of the nobles, the people watching round the place began rioting. Some Jews mixed among the crowd by this means entered the royal doors. Whereat a certain Christian being, it is said, indignant, struck a Jew with his palm and so drove him away from the entrance of the door, thus recalling the king's edict. And many being excited by this example drove away the Jews with insults, and a tumult arising a disorderly crowd came up and believing the king had commanded such treatment, as if relying on the authority of the king, rushed together upon the crowd of Jews waiting at the palace gates. And at first indeed they struck them with the fist but afterwards being more savagely enraged they brought sticks and stones. Then the Jews began to flee, some during their flight being beaten unto death or some of them even being crushed, perished. Now there had come thither with the rest two noble Jews of York, viz., Joce[1] and Benedict, of whom the first escaped, but the other was caught as he fled but tardily from the strokes laid upon him: in order to escape death, he was compelled to confess Christ, and being led into the Church was baptised on the spot.[2] In the meantime a pleasing rumour spread with incredible rapidity through all London, namely that the king had ordered all the Jews to be exterminated. And soon a huge mob of disorderly persons both from the city as well as of those whom the ceremony of the hallowing of the king had attracted from the provinces, run up all armed, and breathing slaughter and spoil against the people by God's judgment hated by all. Then the Jewish citizens, of whom a multitude is known to dwell in London, together with those who had flocked together from all parts withdrew into their own houses. These houses were surrounded by the roaring people, and were stoutly besieged from 9 o'clock till sunset, and as they could not be broken into owing to their strong build[3] and because the madmen had not tools, fire was thrown on the (thatched) roof, and a terrible fire quickly broke out which was fatal to the Jews as they strove (to put it out) and offered the aid of light to the raging Christians at their night work. And the fire kindled against the Jews did not hurt them alone but likewise seized hold of the neighbouring houses of Christians. You might see all of a sudden the best known places of the city wretchedly alight through fires of citizens acting as if they had been enemies. But the Jews were either roasted in their own houses or if they came out of them were received with swords. Much blood was shed in a brief space.[4] But soon the lust after booty burning higher brought on a repletion of slaughter and avarice got the better of cruelty. Thereupon leaving the butchery, their greedy rage betook itself to stripping the houses and snatching their riches. But this in its turn made Christians oppose Christians, for each envied what the other may have seized, and in the eagerness of plunder the rivalry of avarice forgetting all natural ties spared neither friends or comrades.

The new king, however, being of a great and fierce spirit, was indignant and grieved that such things should have occurred at the ceremony of his coronation, and the beginning of his reign. He was angry, and yet perplexed to know what was to be done in the matter. To pass over such a breach of the royal majesty without any example, and to dismiss it unavenged, seemed unworthy of a king and harmful to the state, since passing over such an atrocity would encourage bold and wicked persons to attempt similar misdeeds in confidence of being able to do so with impunity. But on the other hand to exercise the rigour of the royal displeasure against such a multitude of criminals was plainly impossible.[5] For except the nobles banquetting with the King, whose number was such that the breadth of the royal palace seemed narrow, hatred of the Jews and the temptation to plunder had attracted to the perpetration of the deed above-mentioned almost the whole body of the citizens, and almost all the families of the nobles who had come up with the nobles themselves to the ceremony of the King's coronation. He had, therefore to dissemble where vengeance was impossible, God doubtless arranging that those who had stood forth as the ministers of Divine vengeance against blaspheming infidels should not suffer human justice on that account. For the reason of the heavenly example demanded that those blasphemers who in the time of the preceding reign had been too stiff-necked and haughty towards Christians should be humbled at the beginning of its successor. But the prince guaranteed peace to the Jews by an edict after the slaughter; but as will be narrated in its place, they did not enjoy this long, heaven's judgment demanding that the pride of the blaspheming people should be chastised most severely.[6]

William of Newbury *Historia Rerum Anglicanarum*

1. See Chapter 5 Note 2.

2. He was permitted to return to Judaism by Richard I the following day, but died from his wounds shortly afterwards.

3. Jews were amongst the first to build private houses of stone, largely for reasons of security and as protection against fire.

4.	Some 30 Jews were killed, including the eminent Rabbi Jacob of Orleans.

5.	Three Christians were hanged — one for robbing a Christian, and two because the fire they started burnt down a Christian house.

6.	Referring to the 1190 riots in York, Lincoln, Norwich, Lynn, Stamford and Bury St. Edmunds (see Chapter 7).

Fig. 12. A private house of stone c.1190, belonging to Jurnet of Norwich.

Background Reading:

Cecil Roth *A History of the Jews in England* p.18-20.

The York Massacre

The most horrific outbreak of anti-Jewish violence resulting from the preparations for the Third Crusade took place in York.

7.1   1190 The Fate of the Jews of York

But when the King (Richard I) had established himself across the sea many of the province of York plotted against the Jews, not being able to suffer their opulence when they themselves were in need, and without any scruple of Christian conscience thirsting for the blood of infidels from greed for booty. The leaders of this daring plan were some of the nobles indebted to the impious usurers in large sums, some of whom having given up their estates to them for the money they had received, were now oppressed by great want, some bound by their own sureties were pressed by the exactions of the Treasury to satisfy the royal usurers; some, too, of those who had taken the cross and were on the point of starting for Jerusalem were more easily induced to defray the expenses of the journey undertaken for the Lord's sake out of the booty taken from the Lord's enemies, especially as they had little fear of being questioned for the deed when they had started on their journey. One stormy night no small part of the city became on fire either by chance or, as is believed, by arson perpetrated by the conspirators, so that the citizens were occupied with their own houses in fear of the fire spreading. There was nothing, therefore, in the way of the robbers, and an armed band of the conspirators, with great violence and tools prepared for the purpose, burst into the house of Benedict, who had miserably died at London as was mentioned above.[1] There his widow and children with many others dwelt; all of these who were in it were slain and the roof put on fire. And while the fire gloomily increased in strength, the robbers seized their booty and left the burning house, and by help of the darkness retired unobserved and heavy laden. The Jews, and especially their leader Joce[2], in consternation at this misdeed having begged the assistance of the Warden[3] of the royal castle, carried into it huge weights of their monies equal to royal treasures, and removed with their wives and children into the Castle ... But the Warden of the castle having gone out on some business, when he wished to return was not re-admitted by the trembling multitude, uncertain in whom to trust and fearing that perchance his fidelity to them was tottering, and that being bribed he was about to give up to their enemies those whom he should protect. But he immediately went to the sheriff of the county who happened to be at York with a large body of the county soldiers, and complained to him that the Jews had cheated him out of the castle entrusted to him. The sheriff became indignant and raged against the Jews ... and ordered the people to be summoned and the castle to be besieged. The irrevocable word went forth, the zeal of the Christian folk was inflamed, immense masses of armed men both from the town and the country were clustered round the citadel. Then the sheriff struck with regret at his order tried in vain to recall it and wished to prohibit the siege of the castle. But he could by no influence of reason or authority keep back their inflamed minds from carrying out what they had begun.

... Accordingly, the Jews were besieged in the royal tower, and the besieged lacked a sufficient supply of provisions, and would have been quickly starved out by hunger even if no one attacked them from without. But they did not have either a sufficient stock of arms[4] for their own safety or for repelling the enemy.

... When the machines were moved into position, the taking of the Tower became certain, and it was no longer doubtful that the fatal hour was nearing for the besieged. Rabbi Yomtob of Joigny declared: ''God to whom none shall say 'Why dost Thou so?' (Eccles. viii. 4, Dan. iv. 35), orders us to die now for the Law. And behold our death is at the door. Unless, perchance, which God forbid, you think of deserting the sacred Law for this brief space of life, and choose a fate harder than any death to honest and manly minds, namely, to live as apostates at the mercy of impious enemies in the deepest dishonour. Since then we ought to prefer a most glorious death to a very dishonest life, we ought to select the easiest and most honourable form of death. For if we fall into the hands of the enemy we shall die at their will and amidst their jeers. And so since the life which the Creator gave us, He now demands back from us, let us willingly and devoutly render it up to Him with our own hands and let us not await the help of hostile cruelty by giving up what He demands. For many of our people in different times of tribulation are known to have done the same[5], preferring a form of choice most honourable for us.'' When he had said this very many of them embraced his fatal advice, but to many his word seemed a hard one.

... At the order that those men whose courage was most steady should take the life of their wives and pledges, the famous Joce cuts the throat of Anna, his dear wife, with a sharp knife, and did not spare his own sons. And when this had been done by the other men, the fire which had been lighted by them before their death began to burst out in the interior of the tower.

... At daybreak, when the crowd of people collected to storm the castle, those wretched remnants of the Jews standing at the gates declare with tearful voice the slaughter of their people during the night, and, throwing down from their walls their dead bodies as an ocular proof of so great sacrifice, they called out ''Behold the bodies of wretched men who were guilty of their own death with wicked fury and when we refused to do the same but preferred to try Christian clemency, they set fire to the interior of this tower. But God has preserved us both from the madness of our brethren and the danger of the fire so that at last we may be at one with you in religion. For our trouble giving us sense, we recognise the Christian truth and desire its charity being prepared to be laved by the sacred baptism, as you are accustomed to demand and, giving up our ancient rites, to be united to the Christian church. Receive us as brothers instead of enemies, and let us live with you in the faith and ''peace of Christ.'' When they said this with tears many of our men were horrified at the madness of the dead and pitied the survivors. But the leaders of the conspiracy, among whom was a certain Richard Malebysse of a most audacious character, were moved by no pity for these wretches. But speaking fair words to them deceitfully, and promising them the wished for grace with testimony of the faith so that they should not fear to come out, as soon as they did so they seized them as enemies, and though they demanded the baptism of Christ, those cruel butchers destroyed them.

...But when the slaughter was over, the conspirators immediately went to the Cathedral and caused the terrified guardians, with violent threats, to hand over the records of the debts placed there, by which the Christians were oppressed by the royal Jewish usurers, and thereupon destroyed these records of profane avarice in the middle of the church with the sacred fires to release both themselves and many others. Which being done, those of the conspirators who had taken the cross went on their proposed journey before any inquest; but the rest remained in the country in fear of an inquiry.[6] Such were the things that happened at York at the time of the Lord's passion, that is, the day before Palm Sunday (17th March, 1190).

William of Newbury *Historia Rerum Anglicanarum*

1. *See Chapter 6 and Note 2.*
2. *See Chapter 6 and Note 1.*
3. *As the King's representative, it was his duty to protect the King's property, which included the Jews.*
4. *See Chapter 2, Text 2.8.*
5. *In 73 C.E. at Massada, where the Jews committed mass suicide rather than surrender to the Romans.*
6. *150 Jews were reported to have died; the inquiry imposed fines on some 50 burghers.*

Background Reading:

Cecil Roth *A History of the Jews in England* p.22-26.

R. B. Dobson *The Jews of Mediaeval York and the Massacre of March 1190* p.1-48.

Joseph Jacobs *The Jews of Angevin England* p.385-392.

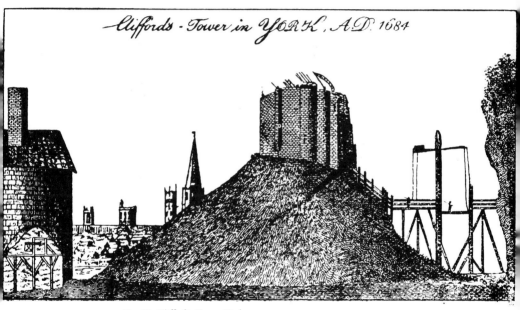

Fig. 13. Clifford's Tower, York

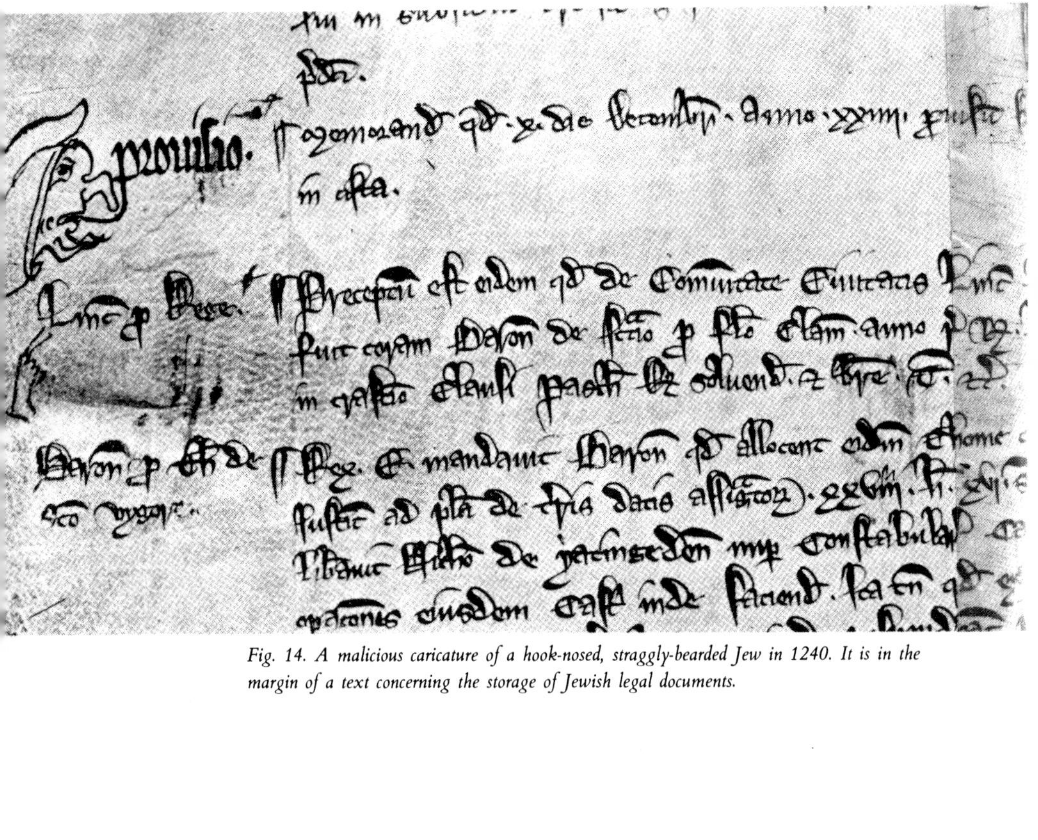

Fig. 14. A malicious caricature of a hook-nosed, straggly-bearded Jew in 1240. It is in the margin of a text concerning the storage of Jewish legal documents.

46

8

Magna Carta

Of the 62 clauses in Magna Carta that the barons forced King John to sign, two related to the Jews. They reflect the moneylending activities of the Jews and their growing unpopularity, and were designed to protect minors and widows from escalating debts.

8.1   1215 Magna Carta

John, by the grace of God, king of England, Lord of Ireland, Duke of Normandy and Acquitaine, Count of Anjou, to the archbishops, bishops, abbots, earls, barons, justiciars, foresters, sheriffs, stewards, servants and all his officials and faithful subjects greeting.

10. If anyone who has borrowed from the Jews any amount, large or small, dies before the debt is repaid, it shall not carry interest as long as the heir is under age, of whomsoever he holds; and if that debt falls into our hands[1], we will take nothing except the principal sum specified in the bond.

11. And if a man dies owing a debt to the Jews, his wife may have her dower and pay nothing of that debt; and if he leaves children under age, their needs shall be met in a manner in keeping with the holding of the deceased; and the debt shall be paid out of the residue, saving the service due to the lords. Debts owing to other than Jews shall be dealt with likewise.

... Given under our hand in the meadow which is called Runnymede between Windsor and Staines on the fifteenth day of June in the seventeenth year of our reign.

1.   *e.g. if the Jewish creditor dies and the king seizes his bonds.*

Background Reading:
Cecil Roth *A History of the Jews in England* p.36-37.

Fig. 15. Aaron, son of Leo, from Colchester, 1277. He stood bail for one of a group of Colchester Jews who were prosecuted under the Law of the Forest for chasing a doe through the streets of the city. He attracted the attention of the Clerk of the Court, who sketched him in the margin of the roll and labelled him 'fil diaboli' (son of the devil). He is wearing the Jew badge.

9

Mandate to the Justices

The long reign of Henry III (1216-1272) saw the decline of mediaeval Anglo-Jewry from a position of relative prosperity to one of complete ruin, buffeted by a rapacious royal policy and an increasingly hostile Church. Their oppressed existence was typified by the Mandate to the Justices:

9.1   **1253 New Restrictions on Jews**

MANDATE OF THE KING TO THE JUSTICES ASSIGNED TO THE CUSTODY OF THE JEWS TOUCHING CERTAIN STATUTES RELATING TO THE JEWS IN ENGLAND WHICH ARE TO BE RIGOROUSLY OBSERVED.

The King has provided and ordained etc.: That no Jew remain in England unless he do the King service, and that from the hour of birth every Jew, whether male or female, serve Us in some way. And that there be no synagogues of the Jews in England save in those places in which such synagogues were in the time of King John, the King's father. And that in their synagogues the Jews, one and all, subdue their voices in performing their ritual offices, that Christians may not hear them. And that all Jews answer to the rector of the church of the parish in which they dwell touching all dues parochial relating to their houses. And that no Christian nurse in future suckle or nourish the male child of any Jew, nor any Christian man or woman serve any Jew or Jewess, or eat with them or tarry in their houses. And that no Jew or Jewess eat or buy meat in Lent. And that no Jew disparage the Christian Faith, or publicly dispute concerning the same. And that no Jew have secret familiar intercourse with any Christian woman, and no Christian man with a Jewess. And that every Jew wear his badge conspicuously on his breast.[1] And that no Jew enter any church or chapel save for purpose of transit, or linger in them in dishonour of Christ. And that no Jew place any hindrance in the way of another Jew desirous of turning to the Christian Faith. And that no Jew be received in any town but by special license of the King, save only in those towns in which Jews have been wont to dwell.

And the Justices assigned to the custody of the Jews are commanded that they cause these provisions to be carried into effect, and rigorously observed on pain of forfeiture of the chattels of the said Jews. Witness the King at Westminster, on the 31st day of January. By King and Council.

1. *Introduced by Pope Innocent III at the 1215 Lateran Council to discourage social relations between Christians and Jews. In England, it took the form of the two tablets of the Ten Commandments.*

Background Reading:
Cecil Roth *A History of the Jews in England* p.58-59.

10

The Statutes of Jewry

Edward I inherited an impoverished Jewry of no further financial benefit to the crown and a powerful Church clamouring for an end to usury. In 1275 he attempted a radical solution to the Jewish problem by issuing Statutes forbidding them to lend money on interest and encouraging them to become merchants, artisans and farmers instead.

10.1   1275 Jews Forbidden To Be Moneylenders

Usury forbidden to the Jews

Forasmuch as the King hath seen that divers Evils, and the disheriting of the good Men of his Land have happened by the Usuries which the Jews have made in Time past, and that divers Sins have followed thereupon; albeit he and his Ancestors have received much benefit from the Jewish People in all Time past; nevertheless for the Honour of God and the common benefit of the People, the King hath ordained and established, That from henceforth no Jew shall lend any Thing at Usury, either upon Land, or upon Rent, or upon other Thing: And that no Usuries shall run in Time coming from the Feast of Saint Edward last past. Notwithstanding, the Covenants before made shall be observed, saving that the Usuries shall cease. But all those who owe Debts to Jews upon Pledges of Moveables, shall acquit them between this and Easter; if not they shall be forfeited. And if any Jew shall lend at Usury contrary to this Ordinance, the King will not lend his Aid, neither by himself nor his Officers, for the recovering of his Loan; but will punish him at his discretion for the Offence, and will do justice to the Christian that he may obtain his Pledge again.

Distresses for Debts to Jews

And that the Distresses[1] for Debts due unto the Jews from

henceforth shall not be so grievous, but that the Moiety[2] of the Lands and Chattels of the Christians shall remain for their Maintenance; and that no Distress shall be made for a Jewry Debt, upon the Heir of the Debtor named in the Jew's Deed, nor upon any other Person holding the Land that was the Debtor's, before that the Debt be put in Suit and allowed in Court.

Valuing of Lands and Goods taken for a Jews' Debt

And if the Sheriff or other Bailiff, by the King's Command hath to give Seisin[3] to a Jew, be it one or more, for their Debt, of Chattels or Land to the Value of the Debt, the Chattels shall be valued by the Oaths of good Men, and be delivered to the Jew or Jews, or to their Proxy, to the Amount of the Debt; and if the Chattels be not sufficient, the Lands shall be extended by the same Oath before the Delivery of Seisin to the Jew or Jews, to each in his due Proportion; so that it may be certainly known that the Debt is quit, and the Christian may have his Land again: Saving always to the Christian the Moiety of his Land and Chattels for his maintenance as aforesaid, and the Chief Mansion.

Warranty to Jews

And if any Moveables hereafter be found in Possession of a Jew, and any Man shall sue him, the Jew shall be allowed his Warranty, if he may have it; and if not, let him answer therefore: So that he be not herein otherwise privileged than a Christian.

Abode of Jews, their badge and their tax

AND that all Jews shall dwell in the King's own Cities and Boroughs, where the Chests of Chirographs of Jewry are wont to be:

Their Badge

And that each jew after he shall be Seven Years old, shall wear a Badge on his outer Garment; that is to say, in the Form of Two Tables joined, of yellow felt, of the Length of Six Inches, and of the Breadth of Three Inches.

Their Tax

And that each one, after he shall be Twelve Years old, pay Three pence yearly at Easter of Tax to the King, whose Bondman he is; and shall hold place as well for a Women as a Man.

Fig. 16. Corbel at Lincoln Cathedral of a bearded Jew, wearing the Jewish badge. Standing above him is a statue of a woman representing the Church Triumphant.

Conveyances of Land, &c. by Jews

And that no Jew shall have Power to infeoff[4] another, whether Jew or Christian, of Houses, Rents, or Tenements that he now hath, nor to alien in any other Manner, nor to make Acquittance to any Christian of his Debt, without the especial Licence of the King, until the King shall have otherwise ordained therein.

53

Privileges of the Jews.

And, Forasmuch as it is the will and sufferance of Holy Church, that they may live and be preserved, the King taketh them under his Protection, and granteth them his Peace; and willeth that they be safely preserved and defended by his Sheriffs and other Bailiffs, and by his Liege Men; and commandeth that none shall do them harm, or damage, or wrong, in their Bodies or in their Goods, moveable or immoveable; and that they shall neither plead nor be impleaded in any Court, nor be challenged or troubled in any Court, except in the Court of the King, whose Bond-men they are. And that none shall owe Obedience, or Service, or Rent, except to the King, or his Bailiffs in his Name; unless it be for their Dwellings which they now hold by paying Rent; saving the Right of Holy Church.

Intercourse between Jews and Christians

And the King granteth unto them that they may gain their living by lawful Merchandise and their Labour; and that they may have Intercourse with Christians, in order to carry on lawful Trade by selling and buying. But that no Christian, for this Cause or any other, shall dwell among them.

Immunity from Scot and Lot

And the King willeth that they shall not by reason of their Merchandise be put to Lot or Scot[5], nor in Taxes with the Men of the Cities or Boroughs where they abide; for that they are taxable to the King as his Bondmen, and to none other but the King.

Holding Houses and Farms, &c.

Moreover the King granteth unto them that they may buy Houses and Curtilages[6], in the Cities and Boroughs where they abide, so that they hold them in chief of the King; saving unto the Lords of the Fee their Services due and accustomed. And that they may take and buy Farms or Land for the Term of Ten Years or less, without taking Homages or Fealties, or such sort of Obedience from Christians, and without having Advowsons of Churches; and that they may be able to gain their living in the World, if they have not the Means of Trading, or cannot

Labour; and this Licence to take Lands to farm shall endure to them only for Fifteen Years from this Time forward[7].

Statutum de Judeismo

1. *Legal seizure of possessions to force the owner to repay debts.*
2. *A half.*
3. *Possession.*
4. *To invest someone with an inherited estate.*
5. *A Tax levied to pay for municipal expenses.*
6. *Small area or yard around a dwelling-house.*
7. *The experiment ended in failure with the majority of Jews unable to find alternative sources of livelihood owing to the economic barriers still in existence and the social antagonism still prevalent between them and their Christian neighbours.*

Fig. 17. Jew in the margin of 1275 manuscript containing the regulation forbidding Jews to practise usury ('Interdicta est iudeis licentia usurandi'). He is wearing the Jewish badge.

By the 13th century, Jewish settlements were to be found throughout England and Wales, although like those of the general population, they were concentrated in the South and East. Towns which had an established Jewish community usually contained archae — special chests under the king's control for the registration of Jewish loans.

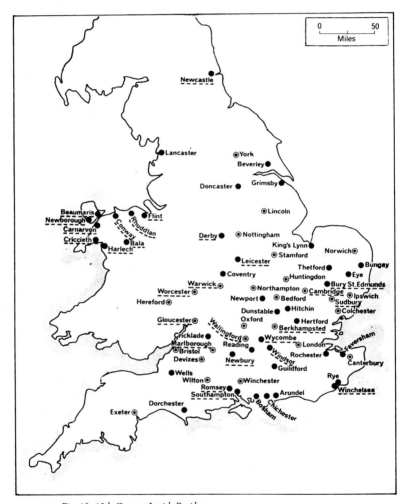

Fig. 18. 13th Century Jewish Residence.

⊙   Towns with archae, in which there was a Jewish community until 1290.
●   Towns without archae, in which Jews lived at some time.
---   Towns from which the Jews were expelled before 1290.

Background Reading:
Cecil Roth *A History of the Jews in England* p.70-76, 256 (also: population distribution p.91-93).
Joseph Jacobs *The Jews of Angevin England* p.373-395 (population distribution).

Fig. 18a. A fragment of letters granting safe conduct for Jews leaving England. 27th July 1290.

11

The Expulsion

When the Statutes of Jewry failed to improve the position of the Jews economically or socially, Edward I decided to solve the problem by expelling the Jews from England altogether. This strategy was also a useful way of pleasing the Church, gaining popular acclaim, and influencing Parliament to vote extra taxes to bolster the royal revenues. The official reason given was that the Jews had secretly engaged in usury and that converts had been persuaded to return to Judaism. There were approximately 3,000 Jews in England at the time. The edict of expulsion is lost, but the writ issued simultaneously to the sheriffs still remains:

11.1 1290 Instructions Concerning The Expulsion

To the sheriff of Gloucester. Whereas the king has prefixed to all the Jews of his realm a certain time[1] to pass out of the realm, and he wills that they shall not be treated by his ministers or others otherwise than has been customary, he orders the sheriff to cause proclamation to be made throughout his bailiwick prohibiting any one from injuring or wronging the Jews within the said time. He is ordered to cause the Jews to have safe-conduct at their cost when they, with their chattels, which the king has granted to them, direct their steps towards London in order to cross the sea[2], provided that before they leave they restore the pledges of Christians in their possession to those to whom they belong[3].

The like to the sheriffs of Essex, York, Northampton, and Lincoln. Also to the sheriff of Hereford and Southampton. At Westminster. The 18th day of July[4].

1. *Before 1st November — the Feast of All Saints.*
2. *The great majority of English Jews settled in France, and nothing further is known of them.*

58

3. *They were allowed to take with them their cash and personal property.*

4. *This corresponded to the Hebrew date, 9th of Av, a fast day that commemorates the destruction of the 1st and 2nd Temples (586 B.C.E. and 70 C.E.) and other tragic events in Jewish history. Thus one more disaster became associated with it.*

Instructions were also sent to the Wardens of the Cinque Ports: (see Fig. 18a for the original letter)

11.2 1290 Safe Conduct for the Jews

The King to all his wardens, officers and sailors of the Cinque Ports, greetings. To each and every Jew of our kingdom we have fixed a definite time-limit for their departure from the kingdom. As we do not wish that they are harmed at all, whether in person or in possession during this period, we place these Jews in your care when they come to the above-mentioned ports with their wives, children and belongings to cross the sea before the aforementioned limit. You should ensure that their passage is safe and speedy, and that their journey, for which they should pay the expense, is free from danger.

In the same way, the poor among the Jews shall be treated sparingly when they come to cross the sea; and for others, according to their ability shall the charge be made, in a restrained fashion according to the type of passage they have. None of them shall be prevented from having passage by excessive or improper demands. We strongly lay upon you this grave responsibility, that no one shall set upon the aforesaid Jews, whether against their person or their possessions in any way, and you shall not permit any injury, molestation, harm or impediment of any kind[5]. At Westminster. 27th day of July.

5. *However, the Channel-crossing itself was very dangerous: some vessels were lost at sea with all on board, while at Queenborough, the captain of a ship enticed the Jews onto a sandbank and then sailed off, leaving them to drown when the tide came in. (He was later tried and hanged).*

THE LONDON JEWRY: 1290.

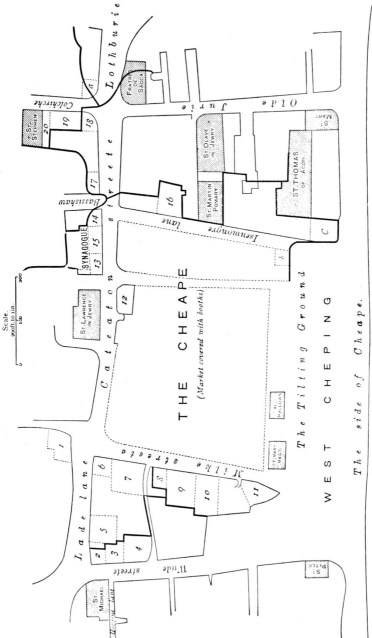

Dark lines indicate Parish Boundaries.

Plots with Numbers belonged to Jews at the Expulsion.

1. Sara Diei.
2. Mosse fil. Elie.
3. Community.
4. Gamaliel de Oxon.
5. Bateman f. Cresse.
6. Roes' Anteman.
7. Mosseus Crispin.
8. Benedict f. Jacob.
9. Jacob f. Bonami.
10. Muriel f. Cresse.

Shadowed buildings represent Churches.

Plots marked by Letters were owned by Jews previous to the Expulsion.

11. Roesia Truyte.
12. Thippe vid. Isaac.
13. Benedict f. Hagin.
14. Manser f. Aaron.
15. Antera vid. Vives.

16. Leo f. Cresse.
17. Elie Fraunceys.
18. Aaron f. Slehme.
19. Jorvin Sackerel.
20. Elie f. Mosse.

a. Earl of Derby, formerly Isaac of Norwich (1214).

b. Earl of Essex, formerly Abraham f. Muriel, formerly Abraham f. Rabbi (1214).

Fig. 19. London Jewry 1290

60

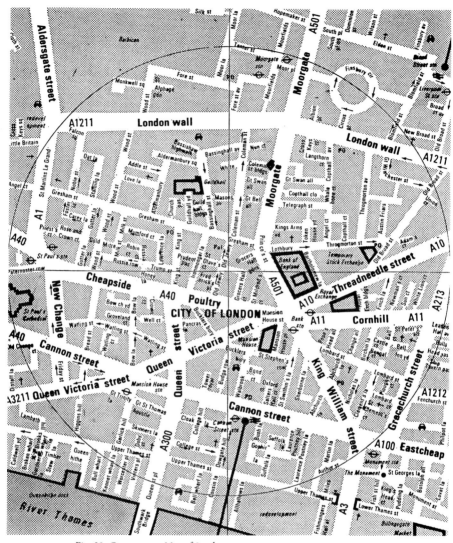

Fig. 20. Contemporary Map of London

Background Reading:

Cecil Roth *A History of the Jews in England* p.85-88.

H. G. Richardson *English Jewry under Angevin Kings* p.213-233.

Fig. 21. Medal struck to commemorate the accession of King Edward VI in 1547, bearing inscriptions in Hebrew and Greek.

12

Marranos in England

When the Jews were expelled from Spain in 1492, many remained there by feigning conversion to Christianity and practising their Judaism in secret. Known as Marranos[1], they were in constant danger of being caught by the Inquisition. Some 40 Marrano families settled in England, although maintaining their disguise, as Jews were still forbidden entry. Their lifestyle is revealed by evidence given by a Marrano to the Milan Inquisition.

12.1   1540 Confession of Gaspar Lopes

Further interrogated he (Gaspar Lopes) said that he knew Alves Lopes in London in whose house he, the deponent, lived for four or five days; and that he, Alves Lopes, holds a Synagogue in his house and lives in the Hebrew manner, though in secret; and that he, the deponent, saw these things and that in this Synagogue they went on one day only[2], the Sabbath; and that on that day there came to Alves's house other false Christians to the number of about twenty; and that it is true that whenever any refugee false Christians come from Portugal to go to England and Flanders and thence to Turkey or elsewhere, in order to lead the lives of Hebrews, they come to the house of the said Alves, who helps them to go whither they want to go for this purpose.

1. *Probably from the Spanish word for 'swine'. Another name for them was Conversos ("the converted ones")*
2. *Instead of everyday to the thrice-daily services.*

Another Marrano, Thomas Fernandes, was forced to give evidence to the Lisbon Inquisition:

And says, that eleven years ago, or thereabouts, finding himself orphaned of both father and mother, he left this city and went to an uncle named Anrique Nuñes, physician, who at the time was living in Bristol, in the kingdom of England, and about a year and a half ago he left Bristol, and has gone, as he is told, to Alvao (?) in France. And upon reaching his said uncle's house, he stayed with him about a year, and did what his uncle told him to do and after being a year in his house, his said uncle — and his wife, who is called Beatriz Fernandes[3] — began to speak to confessant upon certain matters of the old law, previous to which he remembers that both one and the other had said to him that the law of the Jews was good,

... and he observed Saturdays, doing no work on that day, and he likewise observed the fast of Kippur every year while he was in that country, with his said uncle and aunt,

...and so they kept the feast of unleavened bread, eating it on six or seven days. And he remembers that when he, this confessant, was going a sea journey his said aunt put unleavened bread in his provision bag, and told him if there was a storm to throw it into the sea, and the storm would cease; but confessant did not throw it into the sea, only before he was leaving the ship he threw it into the sea so as it might not be seen on shore. And upon some of these festivals they did not work; and his said aunt made the said unleavened bread at home.

And he further remembers that a licentiate named Heitor Nuñes[4], physician, a young unmarried man living in London, sent word every year to his uncle of the days on which Jewish festivals would fall.

...he had worn clean shirts on Saturdays in honour of the Sabbath, and he also remembers that in the house of his uncle as aforesaid they observed other festivals besides that of unleavened bread,

...his aunt, Beatriz Fernandes, of whom he has spoken, was reciting certain Jewish prayers, which she knew by heart, and one Jorge Dias, of whom he has spoken in one of his previous confessions, was writing down the said prayers on paper, and deponent believes that the said Jorge Dias was writing them

Fig. 22. Elizabethan etching of Roderigo Lopez, a Portuguese Marrano, who rose to the
position of medical attendant to Elizabeth I in 1586. However, as the result of a Court
intrigue, he was falsely accused of plotting against the Queen's life and executed in 1594. The
captions mean 'What will you give?' and 'The end of traitors is the rope'.

down in order to say them, and deponent cannot say which prayers they were, because he was never able to learn Jewish prayers, for which reason his said aunt complained of him.

And deponent thinks, but he is not certain of this, that the said Rodrigo da Veiga said to him in London, about three years ago, that he was hoping that tables of the festivals and fasts of the Jews would come from Italy.

...says: That when he was in Bristol, about three years ago, there came there one, Anrique Gonsalves, new Christian, who told this deponent several times that he came from London to Bristol with an aunt of deponent's named Beatriz Fernandes, and deponent's sisters, of whom he has spoken in his confessions, and that he had trouble to find clean things for them to eat in the inns, things which had not been cooked in pans used by Christians, and he gave deponent to understand that they would not eat anything but what Jews are accustomed to eat according to their rites.

3. *Her kinsman, Christopher Fernandes, would send to intercept the spice-ships touching at Southampton and Plymouth, and warn Marranos on board if danger awaited them in Flanders.*
4. *The leader of the Marrano community in London; a skilled physician and an international businessman with widespread contacts, he provided valuable information to the English government in its struggle against Spain.*

Background Reading:
Cecil Roth *A History of the Jews in England* p.135-144.
Cecil Roth *A History of the Marranos* p.252-270.

MERCHANT OF VENICE—Act II., Scene v.

Fig. 23. 19th century engraving of a scene from William Shakespeare's The Merchant of Venice showing Shylock, his daughter Jessica and servant Launcelot Gobbo.

13

Jews in Elizabethan Drama

The two greatest Elizabethan dramatists both wrote plays with a Jew at the centre of the plot, although there were no Jews in England at the time, except the occasional Marrano visitor. Any knowledge of Jews was taken from the Bible, English literature (e.g. Chaucer) and popular mythology. Christopher Marlowe wrote *The Jew of Malta* concerning the attempts of the villainous schemer, Barabas[1], to bring the downfall of his enemies.

13.1   1590 The Jew of Malta

Barabas: We Jews can fawn like spaniels when we please
And when we grin we bite, yet are our looks
As innocent and harmless as a lamb's.

13.2   Barabas

As for myself, I walk abroad a-nights,
And kill sick people groaning under walls:
Sometimes I go about and poison wells;
And now and then, to cherish Christian thieves,
I am content to lose some of my crowns;
That I may, walking in my gallery,
See 'em go pinioned along by my door.
Being young I studied physic, and began
To practise first upon the Italian;
There I enriched the priests with burials,
And always kept the sexton's arms in ure
With digging graves and ringing dead men's knells:
And after that was I an engineer,
And in the wars 'twixt France and Germany,
Under pretence of helping Charles the Fifth,

Slew friend and enemy with my stratagems.
Then after that was I an usurer,
And with extorting, cozening, forfeiting,
And tricks belonging unto brokery,
I filled the jails with bankrouts in a year,
And with young orphans planted hospitals,
And every moon made some or other mad,
And now and then one hang himself for grief,
Pinning upon his breast a long great scroll
How I with interest tormented him.
But mark how I am blest for plaguing them,
I have as much coin as will buy the town.
But tell me now, how hast thou spent thy time?

13.3   **Barabas:** It is no sin to deceive a Christian.

13.4   **Ithamore:** To undo a Jew is charity, and not sin.

> 1.   *It is possible that Marlowe used Dr. Lopez (see Chapter 12) as a model for Barabas, whose character and fate were similar.*

The central theme of William Shakespeare's *The Merchant of Venice* concerns a loan made by Shylock, a Jewish moneylender, to a merchant (a pound of whose flesh would be required if he failed to repay the debt[2]). Although Shylock is the villain of the play, he is at times shown in a sympathetic light.

13.5   **1597 The Merchant of Venice**

Bassanio: If it please you to dine with us.

Shylock: Yes, to smell pork, to eat of the habitation which your prophet the Nazirite[3] conjured the devil into! I will buy with you, sell with you, talk with you, walk with you, and so following; but I will not eat with you, drink with you, nor pray with you.

13.6   **Shylock:** I am a Jew. Hath not a Jew eyes? Hath not a Jew hands, organs, dimensions, senses, affections, passions? — fed with the same food, hurt with the same weapons, subject to the same diseases, healed by the same means, warmed and cooled by the same winter and summer as a Christian is? If you prick us, do we not bleed? If you tickle us, do we not laugh? If you poison us, do we not die? And if you wrong us shall we not revenge?

2.   *Shakespeare's source was an Italian story in which the roles are reversed — a Christian moneylender demands a pound of flesh from a Jewish merchant.*
3.   *See Mark Chapter 5, Verses 1-13.*

Background Reading:

Jacob R. Marcus *The Jew in the Mediaeval World* p.367-372.

Montagu Frank Modder *The Jew in the Literature of England* p.17-30.

Harold Fisch *The Dual Image — A Study of the Jew in English Literature* p.25-38.

Fig. 24. Manasseh ben Israel, an etching by Rembrandt.

14

The Return of the Jews

The rise of the Puritans in the 17th century saw a new attitude towards the Jews. There were several reasons for this development: being a religious minority themselves, the Puritans were more aware of others in a similar situation, such as the Jews; the increased study of the Old Testament led to greater sympathy for present-day Jews; the expectation of the imminent coming of the Messiah gave importance to the role of the Jews and their final conversion; the economic needs of the newly-established Commonwealth made the presence of Jewish merchants desirable; and finally Oliver Cromwell himself was personally well-disposed towards the Jews. Thus there was a considerable public debate on whether to permit the re-admission of the Jews to England. In 1655 the Dutch Rabbi, Manasseh ben Israel, came to London to urge the case and to present his *Humble Address* to Cromwell.

14.1   1655 Jews are Worthy Citizens

Three things, if it please your Highnesse, there are that make a strange Nation well-beloved amongst the Natives of a land where they dwell: (as the defect of those three things make them hatefull) viz. Profit, they may receive from them; Fidelity they hold towards their Princes; and the Noblenes and purity of their blood. Now when I shall have made good, that all these three things are found in the Jewish Nation, I shall certainly persuade your Highnesse, that with a favorable eye (Monarchy being changed into a Republicq), you shall be pleased to receive again the Nation of the Jews, who in time past lived in that Island: but, I know not by what false informations, were cruelly handled and banished.

Profit is a most powerfull motive, and which all the World preferres before all other things and therefore we shall handle that point first.

It is a thing confirmed, that merchandizing is, as it were, the proper profession of the Nation of the Jews. I attribute this in the first place, to the particular Providence and mercy of God towards his people: for having banished them from their own Country, yet not from his Protection, he hath given them, as it were, a naturall instinct, by which they might not only gain what is necessary for their need, but that they should also thrive in Riches and possessions; whereby they should not onely become gracious to their Princes and Lords, but that they should be invited by others to come and dwell in their Lands.

...As for Fidelity, this same affection is confirmed by the inviolable custome of all the Jews wheresoever they live: for on every Sabbath or festivall Day, they every where are used to pray for the safety of all Kings, Princes and Common-wealths, under whose jurisdiction they live, of what profession-soever: unto which duty they are bound by the Prophets and the Talmudists; from the Law, as by Jeremie chap. 29 verse.7. "Seek the peace of the City unto which I have made you to wander: and pray for her unto the Lord, for in her Peace you shall enjoy peace." He speaks of Babylon, where the Jews at that time were captives. From the Talmud ord. 4. tract. 4. Abodazara pereq. 1. "Pray for the peace of the Kingdome, for unlesse there were feare of the Kingdome, men would swallow one the other alive, &c."

...Now, I will not conceale to say, but that alwayes there have bene found some calumniators, that endeavouring to make the Nation infamous, laid upon them three most false reports, as if they were dangerous to the Goods, the Lives, and withall to the very Souls of the Natives. They urge against them their usuries, the slaying of infants to celebrate their Passe-over, and the inducing Christians to become Jews. To all which I shall answer briefly.

1. As for usury, such dealing is not the essential property of the Jews, for though in Germany there be some indeed that practise usury; yet the most part of them that live in Turkey, Italy, Holland and Hamburg, being come out of Spaigne, they hold it infamous to use it; and so with a very small profit of 4. or 5. per Cent, as Christians themselves do, they put their money ordinarily in Banco: for to lay out their money without

any profit, was commanded only toward their brethren of the same Nation of the Jews; but not to any other Nation.

...Our Religion, forbids absolutely the robbing of all men, whatsoever Religion they be of. In our Law it is a greater sinne to rob or defraud a stranger, than if I did it to one of my own profession: because a Jew is bound to shew his charity to all men: for he hath a precept, not to abhorre an Idumean, nor an Egyptian; and that he shall love and protect a stranger that comes to live in his land. If notwithstanding there be some that do contrary to this, they do it not as Jewes simply, but as wicked Jewes, as amongst all nations there are found generally some Usurers.

2. As for killing of the young children of Christians; Whereas the whole world may easily perceive, it is but a meer slander, seeing it is known that at this day, out of Jerusalem, no sacrifice nor blood is in any use by them, even that blood which is found in an Egg is forbidden them, how much more mans blood? But I must not be too prolix; it may suffice to say, that by the Pope himself it was defined in full Counsell the accusation to be false;

3. As for the third Point, it may happen, that some of the Sect of the Papists, of a better mind, embrace the Jewish Religion; it cannot therefore be presumed, that they were induced thereunto by the Jews; seeing the Jews do not entice any man to professe their Law: But if any man of his own free-will come to them, they by their rites & Ceremonies are obliged to make proof of them, whether they come for any temporall interest, and to persuade them to look well to themselves what they do: that the Law unto which they are to submit themselves, is of many precepts; and doth oblige the transgressor to many sore punishments. And so we follow the example of Nahomi, cited in the Sacred Scripture, who did not persuade Ruth to go along with her; but said first to her: Orpa thy sister returned to her Nation and her Gods; go thou and follow her. But Ruth continuing constant, then at length she received her.

Besides this, the Jews indeed have reason to take care for their own preservation; and therefore will not go about by such wayes to make themselves odious to Princes and Common-wealths, under whose Dominions they live.

There were many, however, who opposed the re-admission of the Jews:

14.2   1649 Jews Compete

It's true, they may be usefull where the inhabitants, as in Poland, Spain, and other parts, live in a way of gallantry, affecting War, to drive a trade, but in a countrey abounding with Merchants, natives, they are as water to the shoos: This is not said as against their having their consciences.

Moderate Intelligencer (a Royalist newspaper)

14.3   1649 Jews Accused

No marvell that those which intend to crucifie their King, should shake hands with them that crucified their Saviour.

Mercurius Pragmaticus (a Royalist newspaper)

14.4   1655 Jews Blaspheme

Though perhaps there may not be now in England, any great numbers of professed Jewes (some to my owne knowledge there are, who have their synagogues, and there exercise Judaisme). Yet, they who live here, as often as they are bound to use their office of Prayer (which is twice a day) so often are they bound to blaspheme Christ, and to curse him, and all true Christians which beleeve in him.

Paul Isaiah *The Messias of the Christians*
(originally Eleazar Bargishai, he had converted to Christianity).

14.5   1656 Jews Cheat

The Jewish complexion is so prodigiously timide, as cannot be capable of Armes; for this reason they are no where made Souldiers, nor slaves ... The other impediment is their extreme corrupt love to private interesse; which is notorious in the continuall cheating, and malice among themselves; so as there would want that justice, and respect to common benefit, without which no civill society can stand.

Henry Blount *A Voyage into the Levant*

A formal conference of politicians, lawyers, businessmen and clergy was convened by Cromwell at Whitehall in December 1655 to resolve the issue of re-admission. It ended without a decision. However, in the following year, when the property of the Marrano Antonio Rodrigues Robles, was confiscated as that of an enemy alien, it became clear that as far as the political climate in England was concerned, it was safer to be regarded as an immigrant Jew rather than as a Spanish Catholic. Manasseh ben Israel and various Marranos in London issued a petition openly confessing their Jewish identity.

Fig. 25. Rabbi Manasseh ben Israel presents his petition to Oliver Cromwell. Other characters in the painting are the Lord Chief Justice, Lord Mayor Draper and Mr Secretary Thurloe.

14.6　1656 A Petition[1]

To His Highness Oliver Lord Protector of the Commonwealth of England, Scotland & Ireland & the Dominion thereof.

The Humble Petition of the Hebrews at present Residing in this city of London whose names are underwritten

Humbly shoeweth:

That acknowledging the manyfold favours and Protection your Highness hath been pleased to grant us in order that we may with security meet privately in our particular houses to our Devotions, and being desirous to be favoured more by your Highness we pray with Humbleness that by the best meanes which may be such Protection may be granted us in writing as that we may therewith meet at our private devotions in our particular houses without feare of molestations either to our persons, families or estates, our desires being to live peaceably under your Highness' Government. And being we all mortal, we also humbly pray your Highness to grant us license that those which may die of our nation may be buried in such a place out of this city as we shall think convenient with the proprietors' leave in whose land this place shall be, and so we shall as well in our lifetime, as at our death be highly favoured by your Highness for whose long life and prosperity we shall continually pray to the almighty God.

(Signed) Manasseh ben Israel
David Abrabanel
Abraham Israel Carvajal
Abraham Coen Gonzales
Jahacob de Caceres
Abraham Israel De Brito
Isak Lopez Chillon

1. The original document is pictured on the back cover, along with the note: *Oliver P. Wee doe referr this Peticion to the consideration of ye Councill. March ye 24th 1655/6.*

The reply of the Council of State remains shrouded in mystery, since the pages of the Council Book containing the records for the day it was discussed have been torn out. However, the charges against Robles were withdrawn and his property restored, and by 1657 the Marranos felt confident enough to rent a house for use as a Synagogue: Jewish settlement and rights had been re-established in England without any formal legislation.

Background Reading:
Cecil Roth *A History of the Jews in England* p.149-172.
David S. Katz *Philo-Semitism and the Readmission of the Jews to England 1603-1655.*

Fig. 26. Plaque on the Cunard building in Creechurch Lane in the City of London, marking the site of the Sephardi synagogue established on the readmission of Jews to England under Cromwell.

Fig. 26a. A petition from Menasseh ben Israel and six other London Jews asking Oliver Cromwell for permission to conduct religious services in their private homes, 1656.

The First Synagogues

The first Synagogue of the resettlement was established by Sephardi Jews[1] in 1657 in Creechurch Lane in the City of London. John Greenhalgh, a schoolteacher, visited the Synagogue a few years later and recorded his impressions:

15.1 1662 A Sabbath Service

When Saturday came, I rose very early, the place being far from my lodging; and in a private corner of the City, with much ado, following my directions, I found it at the point of nine o'clock, and was let come in at the first door, but there being no Englishman but myself, and my Rabbi not being there then (for they were but just beginning service) I was at first a little abashed to venture alone amongst all them Jews; but my innate curiosity to see things strange spurring me on, made me confident even to impudence. I rubbed my forehead, opened the inmost door, and taking off my hat (as instructed) I went in and sate me down amongst them; but Lord (Thoma frater) what a strange, uncouth, foreign, and to me barbarous sight was there, I could have wished Thoma that you had then sate next me, for I saw no living soul, but all covered, hooded, guized, veiled Jews, and my own plain bare self amongst them. The sight would have frightened a novice, and made him to have run out again.

Every man had a large white vest, covering, or veil cast over the high crown of his hat, which from thence hung down on all sides, covering the whole hat, the shoulders, arms, sides, and back to the girdle place, nothing to be seen but a little of the face; this, my Rabbi told me, was their ancient garb, used in divine worship in their Synagogues in Jerusalem and in all the Holy Land before the destruction of their City: and though to me at first, it made altogether a strange and barbarous show, yet me thought it had in its kind, I know not how, a face and aspect of venerable antiquity. Their veils were all pure white, made of taffeta or silk, though some few were of a stuff coarser than silk; the veil at each of its four corners had a broad badge; some had red badges, some green, some blue, some wrought with gold or silver, which my Rabbi told me were to distinguish the tribes of which each was common...

Their Synagogue is like a Chapel, high built; for after the first door they go up stairs into it, and the floor is boarded; the seats are not as ours, but two long running seats on either side, as in a school: at the west end of it there is a seat as high as a pulpit, but made deskwise, wherein the two members of the Synagogue did sit veiled, as were all both priest and people. The chief Ruler was a very rich merchant, a big, black, fierce, and stern man to whom I perceive they stand in as reverential an awe as boys to a master; for when any left singing upon their books and talked, or that some were out of tune, he did call aloud with a barbarous thundering voice, and knocked upon the high desk with his fist, that all sounded again. Straight before them, at some distance but on a seat much lower, sate the Priest. Two yards before him, on midst of the floor, stood that whereon the Service and Law were read, being like to an high short table, with steps to it on one side as an altar, covered with a green carpet, and upon that another shorter one of blue silk; two brass candlesticks standing at either end of it; before that on the floor were three low seats whereon some boys sat, their sons, richly veiled, as gentle comely youths as one should see; who had each his Service Book in hand, in Hebrew without points, and were as ready and nimble in it, and all their postures as the men.

There was brought in a pretty Boy at four years old, a child of some chief Jew, in rich coats, with black feathers in his hat, ... he soon leaped off, and ran with his veil dangling up and down; once he came and looked at me, wondering perhaps that I had no veil; at length he got the inner door open and went to his mother; for they do not suffer the women to come into the same room or into the sight of the men: but on the one side of the Synagogue there is a low, long and narrow latticed window, through which the women sitting in the next room, do hear; as the boy opened it, I saw some of their wives in their rich silks bedaubed with broad gold lace, with muffs in one hand and books in the other.

At the east end of the Synagogue standeth a closet like a very high cupboard, which they call the Ark, covered below with one large hanging of blue silk; its upper half covered with several drawing curtains of blue silk; in it are the Books of the Law kept. Before it, upon the floor, stand two mighty brass candlesticks, with lighted tapers in them; from the roof, above the hangings, two great lamps of christal glass, holding each above a pottle filled up to the brim with purest oil, set within a case of four little brass pillars guilded. In the wall at either end of the Synagogue are very many draw boxes, with rings at them like those in a Grocer's Shop; and in it (as I came sooner in the morning than many or most of them) I saw that each Jew at his first entrance into the place did first bow down towards the Ark wherein the Law was kept, but with his hat on, which they never do put off in this place; but a stranger must;

... At last I saw my Rabbi come in. Each Jew after he had bowed went straight to his box, took a little key out of his pocket, unlocked it, took out his veil and books, then threw his veil over his hat and fitted it on all sides, and so went to his place, and fell a tuning it upon his Hebrew Service Book as hard and loud as he could; for all is sung with a mighty noise from first to last, both of priest and people; saying some prayers; and all was done in the right true Hebrew tongue, as my Rabbi affirmed to me afterwards; which, to this end, they do industriously teach all their children from their infancy, having their schoolmistress on purpose, especially their Service books, which they have at their fingers' end...

After this, for a conclusion of all, the Priest read certain select promises of their restoration, at which they showed great rejoicing, by strutting up, so that some of their veils flew about like morris dancers, only they wanted bells. This forenoon service continued about three hours, from nine to twelve, which being ended, they all put off their veils, and each man wrapping his veil up, went and put it and his Hebrew Service Book into his box, and locking it departed.

My Rabbi invited me afterwards to come and see the feast of

Fig. 27. The interior of Bevis Marks, London, the oldest synagogue in Britain, built 1701.

Purim, which they kept he said for the deliverance from Haman's Conspiracy, mentioned in the Book of Esther; in which they use great knocking and stamping when Haman is named. Also he desired me to come and see them at the Passover, which they did ten days before our Easter, and he had got me to the door of the place, but I felt such a reluctancy in me, ... So I came away back again without seeing it; though afterwards I understood that several had been there to see them eat it, who brought away some of their unleavened bread with them, and showed to some who told me. One year in Oliver's time, they did build booths on the other side of Thames, and kept the Feast of Tabernacles in them, as some told me who saw them; but since the King's coming in, they are very close, nor do admit any to see them but very privately.

When I was in the Synagogue I counted about or above a hundred right Jews, one proselite amongst them, they were all gentlemen (merchants) I saw not one mechanic person of them; most of them rich in apparel, divers with jewels glittering (for they are the richest jewellers of any). They are all generally black so as they may be distinguished from Spaniards or native Greeks, for the Jews hair hath a deeper tincture of a more perfect raven black, they have a quick piercing eye, and look as if of strong intellectuals; several of them are comely, gallant, proper gentlemen. I knew many of them when I saw them daily upon the Exchange and the Priest there too, who also is a merchant.

1. *Jews originating from Spain and Portugal.*

The diarist Samuel Pepys also visited the Creechurch Lane Synagogue and attended the Festival of Simchat Torah (the Rejoicing of the Law):

15.2   1663 A Disorderly Service

After dinner my wife and I, by Mr. Rawlinson's conduct, to the Jewish Synagogue: where the men and boys in their vayles, and the women behind a lattice out of sight; and some things stand up, which I believe is their Law, in a press to which all coming in do bow; and at the putting on their vayles do say something, to which others that hear him do cry Amen, and the party do kiss his vayle. Their service all in a singing way, and in Hebrew. And anon their Laws that they take out of the press are carried by several men, four or five several burthens in all, and they do relieve one another; and whether it is that every one desires to have the carrying of it, I cannot tell, thus they carried it round about the room while such a service is singing. And in the end they had a prayer for the King, which they pronounced his name in Portugall; but the prayer, like the rest, in Hebrew. But, Lord! to see the disorder, laughing, sporting, and no attention, but confusion in all their service, more like brutes than people knowing the true God, would make a man forswear ever seeing them more: and indeed I never did see so much, or could have imagined there had been any religion in the whole world so absurdly performed as this[2]. Away thence with my mind strongly disturbed with them, by coach and set down my wife in Westminster Hall.

Diary of Samuel Pepys

2. *Whereas decorum is the rule for most services, Simchat Torah is a time of exuberance and high spirits.*

The first Ashkenazi community (Jews from Central Europe) was established in 1690 and the community's first Synagogue, The Great Synagogue, was built in 1722. It was enlarged and remodelled in 1790, but destroyed during a bombing raid in 1941.

Background Reading:
R. D. Barnett and A. Levy *The Bevis Marks Synagogue.*
Cecil Roth *The Great Synagogue, London 1690-1940.*

Fig. 28. "The Great Synagogue, Duke's Place" 1809. A close examination reveals some caricature-like elements.

16

The Jew Bill

A difficulty facing Jews born abroad who settled in England was the lengthy and costly procedure involved in becoming naturalized. Without naturalization Jews could not own land and ships, or trade with the plantations. The issue was brought to the public attention by the radical free-thinker John Toland, who urged a more liberal attitude.

16.1   1714 Naturalized Jews Would Be An Asset

Tis manifest almost at first sight, that the common reasons for a GENERAL NATURALIZATION, are as strong in behalf of the Jews, as of any other people whatsoever. They encrease the number of hands for labor and defence, of bellies and backs for consumtion of food and raiment, and of brains for invention and contrivance, no less than any other nation. We all know that numbers of people are the true riches and power of any country.

My Purpose at present then, is to prove, that the Jews are so farr from being an Excresence or Spunge (as some wou'd have it) and a useless member in the Commonwealth, or being ill subjects, and a dangerous people on any account, that they are obedient, peaceable, useful, and advantageous as any; and even more so than many others: for being excluded every where in Europe, from publick Employments in the State, as they are from following Handycraft-trades in most places, and in almost all, from purchasing immovable Inheritances, this does no less naturally, than necessarily, force 'em to Trade and Usury, since otherwise they cou'd not possibly live. Yet let 'em once be put upon an equal foot with others, not only for buying and selling, for security and protection to their Goods and Persons; but likewise for Arts and Handycraft-trades, for purchasing and inheriting of estates in Lands and Houses (with which they may as well be trusted as with Shares in the publick Funds) and then I doubt not, but they'll insensibly betake themselves to Building, Farming, and all sorts of Improvement like other people.

We deny not that there will thus be more taylors and shoomakers; but there will also be more suits and shoos made than before. If there be more weavers, watchmakers, and other artificers, we can for this reason export more cloth, watches, and more of all other commodities than formerly: and not only have 'em better made by the emulation of so many workmen, of such different Nations; but likewise have 'em quicker sold off, for being cheaper wrought than those of others, who come to the same market. This one Rule of MORE, and BETTER, and CHEAPER, will ever carry the market against all expedients and devices.

John Toland *Reasons for Naturalizing the Jews of Great Britain and Ireland*

A bill was eventually passed simplifying the procedure and allowing foreign Jews to be naturalized after three years' residence in England. However, the right of naturalization was limited to persons of property and the richer classes, and the bill prohibited purchases that gave the owner control over any ecclesiastical office:

16.2 1753 'The Jew Bill'

Whereas by an Act made in the Seventh year of the reign of King James the First, intituled, An Act that all such as are to be naturalized or restored in Blood, shall first receive the Sacrament of the Lord's Supper, and the Oath of Allegiance, and the Oath of Supremacy, every person who shall apply to be naturalized by Act of Parliament, being of the Age of Eighteen Years or upwards, is required to receive the Sacrament of the Lord's Supper, within One Month before such Naturalization is exhibited, whereby many Persons of considerable Substance professing the Jewish Religion, are prevented from being naturalized by Bill to be exhibited in Parliament for that Purpose: And whereas by an Act made in the Thirteenth Year

Fig. 29. What will befall State and Church after the passing of the Naturalization Bill. A contemporary cartoon.

of his present Majesty's Reign, intituled, An Act for
Naturalizing such Foreign Protestants, and others therein
mentioned, as are settled, or shall settle in any of his Majesty's
Colonies in America[1], Persons professing the Jewish Religion,
are naturalized upon their complying with the terms therein
mentioned, without their receiving the Sacrament of the Lord's
Supper; Be it therefore enacted by the King's most excellent
Majesty, by and with the Advice and consent of the Lords
Spiritual and Temporal, and Commons, in this present
Parliament assembled, and by the Authority of the same, That
Persons professing the Jewish Religion may, upon Application
for that Purpose, be naturalized by Parliament, without
receiving the Sacrament of the Lord's Supper, the said Act of
the Seventh Year of the Reign of King James the First, or any
other Law, Statute, Matter or Thing to the contrary in any
ways notwithstanding

And it is hereby further enacted by the Authority aforesaid,
That from and after the First Day of June, one thousand seven
hundred and fifty-three, every Person professing the Jewish
Religion shall be disabled, and is hereby made incapable to
purchase, either in his or her own name, or in the Name of any
other Person or Persons, to his or her Use, or in Trust for him
or her, or to inherit or take by Descent, Devise, or Limitation,
in Possession, Reversion, or Remainder, any advowson or
Right of Patronage, or Presentation, or other Right or interest
whatsoever of, in, or to any Benefice, Prebend, or other
Ecclesiastical Living or Promotion, School, Hospital, or
Donative whatsoever.

The Jewish Naturalization Act

1. The Plantation Act

Despite being of little consequence, it aroused widespread
protests and became known as 'the Jew Bill'. Reflecting the
popular concern, the London Magazine published reports from an
imaginary Hebrew journal on what life would be like a century
later when the Jews were in control:

We are informed that the statue of Sir John Barnard[2], formerly father of this City, and a strenuous asserter of Christianity, is ordered to be taken down, and that of Pontius Pilate is to be put up in his place ... Last night the bill for naturalizing Christians was thrown out of the Sanhedrin by a great majority ... the good ship Rodrique, alias Salvador, Jewish built is now at Limehouse ready to take those Christian families that may be inclined to transport themselves to Turkey, choosing to live under a Mahommedian rather than a Jewish government ... On Wednesday last, died the Duke of Hebron, in Berkshire, Sir Nadab Issachar, Attorney-General; he is succeeded in office by Moses da Costa ... Jewish services are held daily at the London Synagogue, formerly St. Paul's ... Trade continues to decline following the introduction of a second Sabbath-day in every week ... The importation of pork has now become a penal offence.

The London Magazine

2.   *A vehement opponent of the Bill in 1753.*

The popular furore was so great that in December 1753 the government of the Duke of Newcastle repealed the Act after only eight months on the statute books. The position of English-born Jews was not affected by the affair as they were English subjects with full rights concerning land and trade.

Background Reading:
Cecil Roth *A History of the Jews in England* p.216-223.
James Picciotto *Sketches in Anglo-Jewish History* p.82-91.

17

The Board of Deputies

When George III came to the throne, the Sephardi community appointed seven deputies to present a loyal address to the new monarch.

17.1   1760 A Loyal Address

The Portugese Jews most humbly begged leave to condole with his Majesty on the demise of the late king, whose sacred memory would ever be revered, and to congratulate his Majesty on his accession to the throne of these kingdoms; humbly craving the continuance of his Majesty's favour and protection, which they hope to merit by an unalterable zeal for his Majesty's most sacred person and service, and by promoting to the utmost of their abilities the benefit of his Majesty's realms.

When the leaders of the Ashkenazi community reproached the leaders of the Sephardi community for having acted independently, they agreed to co-operate in such matters in future and to establish the London Committee of Deputies of the British Jews:

17.2   1760 United Action

Resolved that whenever any public affair should occur that may interest the two nations, we will on our parts communicate to the Committee of the Dutch[1] Jews' Synagogue what we think proper should be done, and we desire the same gentlemen may do the same, and make a minute thereof.

1.   i.e. Ashkenazi Jews — probably a corruption of Deutsch (German).

The Committee remained a largely passive organisation until Moses Montefiore became President in 1835. In the following year, the first constitution was formally drawn up:

Fig. 30. Signing the loyal address on the coronation of George III. A contemporary cartoon.

17.3 **1836 The Board of Deputies**

1. That this Meeting is convinced it would be of essential advantage to the interests of the Jews of Britain, that in all matters touching their political welfare they should be represented by one Body, and inasmuch as the general Body of Deputies have long been recognized as their representatives, it is highly desirable for the general good that all the British Jews should so acknowledge them, having a sufficient number of Members from each Congregation to ensure the accordance of their proceedings with the general wishes of the Jews.

2. That this Body be intitled 'Deputies of the British Jews', and composed of the following Members:-

7 Deputies from the Portuguese Synagogue.
7 Deputies from the Great Synagogue
4 Deputies from the Hambro Synagogue
4 Deputies from the New Synagogue

3. That in all cases which may tend to protect and promote the welfare of the Jews, the Deputies shall be authorized to adopt such measures as they may deem proper, in order to obtain such objects.

10. That whenever any of the Congregation of Jews in the United Kingdom shall be desirous of sending their Deputies for the purpose of uniting with this Body, such Deputies shall be admitted as part of the Deputies of the British Jews, and shall be required to furnish such proportion of the Expenses as shall be considered equitable.

Minute Book of the Board of Deputies

Fig. 31. Etching (1883) depicting the career of Moses Montefiore. 1) Captain of Surrey Militia, 1805. 2) Carrying dispatches of the battle of Navarino (1827). 3) First visit to the East, 1827. 4) Presented to Mehemet Ali in Egypt. 5) Meeting Emperor Nicholas of Russia. 6) Travelling in the desert.

Under Montefiore's leadership, the Board's activities were extended to defending Jewish rights world-wide. The most infamous case was the Damascus Blood Libel of 1840, following which Montefiore received supporters to his coat of arms from Queen Victoria as a mark of favour:

Victoria, by the grace of God, etc., etc.,

Whereas it has been represented unto us that our trusty and well beloved Sir Moses Montefiore, of Grosvenor Gate, Park Lane, in the Parish of St. George, Hanover Square, in our county of Middlesex, and of East Cliff Lodge, Ramsgate, in our county of Kent, Knight, Fellow of the Royal Society, and later Sheriff of London and Middlesex, in consequence of information having been received from the East that a number of Jews have been imprisoned and tortured at Damascus and at Rhodes, and that many children had been imprisoned and almost deprived of food and several persons tortured till they died, under the plea that the Jews had assassinated a priest called Father Thomas at Damascus; he had in conformity to a voluntary offer made at a general meeting of the London Committee of Deputies of the British Jews and others, held on the 15th of June last, proceeded (accompanied by Lady Montefiore) to Alexandria with the view of proving the falsity of the accusation, and of advocating the cause of his unfortunate and persecuted brethren, that he arrived at Alexandria in the beginning of August and succeeded in obtaining from the Pasha of Egypt, Mahommed Ali, the release with honour of the persons accused who had been confined, and permission for those who had fled to return to their homes, and he then proceeded to where he had an audience with the Sultan, Abdoul Medjid, and obtained from his Imperial Majesty a Firman proclaiming the innocence of the Jews, and securing to all persons professing the Jewish religion under the Turkish dominion, equal rights with their fellow subjects.

We, taking the premises into our Royal consideration, and being desirous of giving a special mark of our Royal favour to the said Sir Moses Montefiore in commemoration of these his unceasing exertions in behalf of his injured and persecuted brethren in the East and of the Jewish nation at large, have been graciously pleased to allow him to bear supporters, although the privilege of bearing supporters be limited to the Peers of our Realm, the Knights of our Orders and the Proxies of Princes of our Blood at installations, except in such cases wherein, under particular circumstances, we have been pleased to grant on a licence for the use thereof, etc., etc., etc.

Given at our Court at St. James's, the 24th of June in the fifth year of our reign.

On the Dexter side, Lion guardant, and on the Sinister side, a Stag, each supporting a Flagstaff, therefrom flowing a Banner to the dexter, inscribed 'Jerusalem' in Hebrew characters.

Fig. 32.
Coat of Arms of
Sir Moses Montefiore.

Today the Board is the central organisation for all aspects of Anglo-Jewish life, particularly civil and political rights. It is made up of representatives of all Synagogues in Britain. It includes a Statistical and Demographic Unit, whose most recent report was issued in 1983:

17.5   **Estimated Population of British Jewry by Age and Sex in 1977**

Table 1	Total		Sex Ratios
Age Group	Males	Females	Male:Female
0-9	23,190	21,880	1.06
10-19	26,210	24,960	1.05
20-34	37,340	36,250	1.03
35-44	19,170	18,610	1.03
45-54	20,130	20,330	0.99
55-64	19,930	21,900	0.91
65-74	16,940	22,290	0.76
75-84	6,850	13,690	0.50
85 and over	1,200	2,850	0.42
TOTAL	170,960	182,760	0.93
	353,720		

Comparative Age Structures

Table 2

Age Group	Estimated British Jewish Population 1975-9	England & Wales Population 1975-9
0-9	12.7	14.0
10-19	14.5	15.8
20-34	20.8	21.1
35-44	10.7	11.5
45-54	11.4	11.8
55-64	11.8	11.3
65-74	11.1	9.2
75-84	5.8	4.3
85 and over	1.2	1.0
TOTAL	100.0%	100.0%

The Size and Structure of British Jewry in 1977.

Fig. 33. Meeting of the Board of Deputies 1967.

Background Reading:

Cecil Roth *A History of the Jews in England* p.224-225, 258-259.

Chaim Bermant *Troubled Eden* p.97-106.

Louis Loewe *Diaries of Sir Moses and Lady Montefiore* p.208-300 (The Damascus Blood Libel).

97

18

Emancipation

Despite having full social and economic emancipation, Anglo-Jewry lacked many political rights, as the oaths of office all involved the phrase "upon the true faith of a Christian". The struggle to gain entry to Parliament started in 1830, but a Bill in favour of Jewish emancipation was defeated in the House of Commons. Lord Macaulay spoke forcefully on behalf of the Jews in subsequent debates:

18.1   1833 Plea for Jewish Rights

The Jew may be a juryman, but not a judge. He may decide issues of fact, but not issues of law. He may give a hundred thousand pounds damages; but he may not in the most trivial case grant a new trial. He may rule the money-market: he may influence the exchanges: he may be summoned to congresses of Emperors and Kings. Great potentates, instead of negotiating a loan with him by tying him in a chair and pulling out his grinders, may treat with him as with a great potentate, and may postpone the declaring of war or the signing of a treaty till they have conferred with him. All this is as it should be: but he must not be a Privy Councillor. He must not be called Right Honourable, for that is political power. And who is it that we are trying to cheat in this way? Even Omniscience. Yes, Sir; we have been gravely told that the Jews are under the divine displeasure, and that if we give them political power God will visit us in judgment. Do we then think that God cannot distinguish between substance and form? Does not He know that, while we withhold from the Jews the semblance and name of political power, we suffer them to possess the substance?

... In one important point, Sir, my honourable friend, the Member for the University of Oxford[1], must acknowledge that the Jewish religion is of all erroneous religions the least mischievous. There is not the slightest chance that the Jewish religion will spread. The Jew does not wish to make proselytes. He may be said to reject them. He thinks it almost culpable in one who does not belong to his race to presume to belong to his religion. It is therefore not strange that a conversion from Christianity to Judaism should be a rarer occurrence than a total eclipse of the sun. There was one distinguished convert in the last century, Lord George Gordon[2]; and the history of his conversion deserves to be remembered. For if ever there was a proselyte of whom a proselytising sect would have been proud, it was Lord George; not only because he was a man of high birth and rank; not only because he had been a member of the legislature;

...But was he allured into the synagogue? Was he even welcomed to it? No, Sir; he was coldly and reluctantly permitted to share the reproach and suffering of the chosen people;

...The honourable Member for Oldham[3] tells us that the Jews are naturally a mean race, a sordid race, a money-getting race; that they are averse to all honourable callings; that they neither sow nor reap; that they have neither flocks nor herds; that usury is the only pursuit for which they are fit; that they are destitute of all elevated and amiable sentiments. Such, Sir, has in every age been the reasoning of bigots. They never fail to plead in justification of persecution the vices which persecution has engendered. England has been to the Jews less than half a country; and we revile them because they do not feel for England more than a half patriotism. We treat them as slaves, and wonder that they do not regard us as brethren. We drive them to mean occupations, and then reproach them for not embracing honourable professions. We long forbade them to possess land; and we complain that they chiefly occupy themselves in trade.

1.   Sir Robert Inglis. He had also opposed the Repeal of the Test and Corporation Acts in 1828, which removed the political disabilities of the Nonconformists.
2.   He had converted to Judaism in 1787, but was shunned by the Jewish community.
3.   William Cobbett.

Fig. 34. Cartoon published in 1829 showing the Jews trying to enter Parliament, the Catholics having already gained entry.

Further Bills to gain the entry of Jews into Parliament were passed in the House of Commons, but were always defeated in the House of Lords. Consequently, energies were channelled into winning municipal rights instead. These were achieved in the Jewish Disabilities Removal Act:

Whereas the Declaration prescribed by an Act of the Ninth Year of the Reign of King George the Fourth, intituled An Act for repealing so much of several Acts as imposes, 'the Necessity of receiving the Sacrament of the Lord's Supper as a Qualification for certain Offices and Employments, upon Admission into Office in Municipal Corporations, cannot conscientiously be made and subscribed by Persons of the Jewish Religion:' Be it therefore enacted by the Queen's most Excellent Majesty, by and with the Advice and Consent of the Lords Spiritual and Temporal, and Commons, in this present Parliament assembled and by the Authority of the same, That, instead of the Declaration required to be made and subscribed by the said recited Act, every Person of the Jewish Religion be permitted to make and subscribe the following Declaration within One Calendar Month next before or upon his Admission into the Office of Mayor, Alderman, Recorder, Bailiff, Common Councilman, Councillor, Chamberlain, Treasurer, Town Clerk, or any other Municipal Office in any City, Town Corporate, Borough, or Cinque Port, within England and Wales or the Town of Berwick-upon-Tweed:

I A. B., being a Person professing the Jewish Religion, having conscientious Scruples against subscribing the Declaration contained in an Act passed in the Ninth Year of the Reign of King George the Fourth, intituled An Act for repealing so much of several Acts as imposes the Necessity of receiving the Sacrament of the Lord's Supper as a Qualification for certain Offices and Employments, do solemnly, sincerely, and truly declare, That I will not exercise any Power or Authority or Influence which I may possess by virtue of the Office of ... to injure or weaken the Protestant Church as it is by Law established in England, nor to disturb the said Church, or the Bishops and Clergy of the said Church, in the Possession of any Right or Privileges to which such Church or the said Bishops and Clergy may be by Law entitled.'

The battle returned to Parliament. Baron Lionel de Rothschild was twice elected for Parliament by the City of London, but was unable to take up his seat because of the oath. A more aggressive approach was adopted by Sir David Salomons when elected for Greenwich. He took his seat without saying the full oath, made a speech and voted in three divisions:

18.3   1851 Salomons Causes An Uproar

In the middle of the House of Commons stood a peculiarly mild and gentleman-like man, looking as much like a quiet and cultivated country gentleman as the majority of Members surrounding him. Round this calm and smiling personage a war of parliamentary elements were raging loud and fierce. Amid shouts of 'Withdraw' from one side and loud cheers from the other, the hon. Member somehow gained the ear of the House. The favour of a large body of the House, the winning aspect of the intruder, the curiosity prevailed. There was a pause and then amid breathless silence Mr Alderman Salomons delivered his maiden speech.

Sir ... I trust the House will make some allowance for the novelty of my position, and the responsibility I feel for the unusual course which it may be thought I had adopted. But having been returned to this House by a large majority ... I thought I should not be doing justice to my position as an Englishman and a gentleman did I not adopt the course which I thought right and proper of maintaining my right to appear on the floor ... and stating before the House and the country what I believe to be my rights and privileges ... I hope this House will not refuse what I believe no court in the country refuses the meanest subject of the realm — that it will not refuse to hear me before it comes to a final decision.

Loud cheers succeeded the silence of expectancy with which the speech was listened to, and Lord John Russell, having complimented the Member for Greenwich on the calmness of his address, the debate was continued.

Although Salomons was forced to withdraw, continual pressure eventually resulted in the Jewish Relief Act, which removed all obstacles:

Fig. 35. Sir David Salomons.

18.4   1858 Parliament Opened To Jews

Be it enacted by the Queen's most Excellent Majesty, by and with the Advice and Consent of the Lords Spiritual and Temporal, and Commons, in this present Parliament assembled, and by the Authority of the same, as follows:

I. Where it shall appear to either House of Parliament that a Person professing the Jewish Religion, otherwise entitled to sit and vote in such House, is prevented from so sitting and voting by his conscientious Objection to take the Oath which by an

Act passed or to be passed in the present Session of Parliament has been or may be substituted for the Oaths of Allegiance, Supremacy, and Abjuration in the Form therein required, such House, if it think fit, may resolve that thenceforth any Person professing the Jewish Religion, in taking the said Oath to entitle him to sit and vote as aforesaid, may omit the Words "and I make this Declaration upon the true Faith of a Christian."

III. Nothing herein contained shall extend or be construed to extend to enable any Person or Persons professing the Jewish Religion to hold or exercise the Office of Guardians and Justices of the United Kingdom, or of Regent of the United Kingdom, under whatever Name, Style, or Title such Office may be constituted, or of Lord High Chancellor, Lord Keeper or Lord Commissioner of the Great Seal of Great Britain or Ireland, or the Office of Lord Lieutenant or Deputy or other Chief Governor or Governors of Ireland, or Her Majesty's High Commissioner to the General Assembly of the Church of Scotland.

IV. Where any Right of Presentation to any Ecclesiastical Benefice shall belong to any Office in the Gift or Appointment of Her Majesty, Her Heirs or Successors, and such Office shall be held by a Person professing the Jewish Religion, the Right of Presentation shall devolve upon and be exercised by the Archbishop of Canterbury for the Time being; and it shall not be lawful for any Person professing the Jewish Religion, directly or indirectly, to advise Her Majesty, Her Heirs or Successors, or any Person or Persons holding or exercising the Office of Guardians of the United Kingdom, or of Regent of the United Kingdom, under whatever Name, Style, or Title such Office may be constituted, or the Lord Lieutenant or Lord Deputy, or any other Chief Governor or Governors of Ireland, touching or concerning the Appointment to or Disposal of any Office or Preferment in the United Church of England and Ireland, or in the Church of Scotland; and if such Person shall offend in the Premises he shall, being thereof convicted by due Course of Law, be deemed guilty of a high Misdemeanor, and disabled for ever from holding any Office, Civil or Military, under the Crown.

Baron Lionel de Rothschild became the first Jewish M.P. in the same year. Within two years there were three other Jews in Parliament, including Sir David Salomons (who had become the first Jewish Lord Mayor of London in 1855). Amid the celebrations within Anglo-Jewry, there were also some cautionary voices:

18.5 1861 A Matter of Opinion

Every movement and every vote of theirs will be identified with the community, and the latter morally held responsible for their public acts. ...

What if it should be our misfortune to be represented by men only nominally Jews ... without Jewish feeling, and without Jewish conviction ... Would it not be better for the Jewish community not to have any of its members in Parliament than to be represented by men of this kind?

The Jewish Chronicle

A more positive view was presented by the general press when seven Jews were returned in the election of 1868:

18.6 1868 We Are Nineteen

Twelve Jolly Quakers, or those who were such,
Are elected M.P. not a Quaker too much.
Twelve jolly Quakers, and Seven jolly Jews,
Were the right sort of birds for electors to choose.
For none than a Quaker's more ready to fight,
When he thinks, as he usually does, that he's right,
And none more than a Jew is more ready to pay,
When he sees that the money will go the right way;
And when our War-Estimates come, will come too
The pluck of the Quaker, the sense of the Jew.
We look to them both, though the Colonels may storm,
For liberal provision, but searching reform.
So hooray for the voters with wisdom to choose
Our Twelve Jolly Quakers, and Seven Jolly Jews!

Punch

Fig. 36. Baron Lionel de Rothschild taking his seat in the House of Commons.

Background Reading:

Cecil Roth *A History of the Jews in England* p.241-266.

Cecil Roth "Lord George Gordon's Conversion to Judaism" in *Essays and Portraits in Anglo-Jewish History* p.183-210.

Geoffrey Alderman *The Jewish Community in British Politics* p.14-30.

M. C. N. Salbstein *The Emancipation of the Jews in Britain.*

19

Everyday Life in the 18th and 19th Centuries

The readmission of the Jews to England not only brought rights of settlement but also resulted in a high degree of social and cultural integration of the Jews. At a time when their European co-religionists still had to live in ghettos, endure poll taxes and face popular hostility, English Jews moved freely in general society.

19.1   **1735 Jews and Society**

'The Jews are estimated as amounting to about 6,000 souls. They possess houses and villas, in which they either dwell or lease to each other. Many of them ride in carriages, and there are some of them who are wealthy ... Jews may dwell in any part of the City where they wish. They may practise any sort of trade or craft and open a shop in any place outside the City in the suburbs, and even in the City if they have practised the craft seven years under a master, in the same way as a Protestant may, the limits being those fixed for the City.

'They do not become excited in matters of religion and everyone who is observant is held in good repute, and when occasion arises each may speak his mind without concern or fear of being indicted, just as one may speak about the King, as it seems.

'The Jews have Protestants in their employ as maid-servants, waiters, servants, and coachmen, even as wet-nurses, and entrust to them without any trouble their own little children to be brought up, the suspicion that they might baptise them never occurring to them. It has never occurred, and if it should, they would be severely punished, and such a baptism would be held invalid. So without concern they send their little girls to Protestant women teachers, and little boys to Protestant teachers, to acquire manners and good qualities and learning. Some possess these assets and are very famous doctors and surgeons, held in great esteem, others are doctors of laws and notaries, who command public confidence, and their notarial deeds are accepted equally with those of Protestants. One hears of no mockery or abuse of Jews as in other countries, where there is a certain vulgar weakness for persecuting and regarding Hebrews as something abominable who should be differentiated from the rest by Catholic law and be despised without distinction of case, terms, occasion, or quality of persons. . . .

'There is no discrimination between Jew and Protestant in burdens or taxes. All alike discharge guard duties in the City; it falls turn and turn about on the heads of households, in which even the great are included, and they can all alike serve as constables and bear the King's arms, differing only by religion, which is not discussed. Each one is esteemed in terms of his action and behaviour as a gentleman, which is what they most esteem.

'I saw during this time two Protestants becoming Jews and be circumcised, and two ladies likewise embrace the Jewish religion with great devotion. The difficulties that the Jews themselves place in the way of those who wish to become Jews are so great that it would seem impossible that anyone should resolve to take such a step. But when it is resolved, it is not taken for an ulterior motive but because they believe that infallibly they are doing rightly. After all the warnings to proselytes, when nothing remains but the act of circumcision, and the operation is to be performed, they bring out a great knife, like that with which the Jews slaughter cattle, which would put fear in a giant, shining like crystal, then the brave fellows resign themselves to endure the pain in order to embrace the Hebrew religion and to believe in the Hebrew Law as the true Law.

'Some marriages take place where the husband and the wife are of different religions; of such the male children belong to the husband and the female to the wife, and when they reach an age when they are capable of distinguishing, each may choose that religion which is or she desires. There are even Hebrews with Protestant wives among them. It happened one day that the Wardens of the Community were at the Bishop's house. He asked them if the Jews had any shortage of women that they had need of marrying Protestants'.

The Travels of Moses Cassuto

Fig. 37. An English Jew, David Moses Dyte, prevents the assassination of George III at the Drury Lane Theatre 15th May 1800.

Despite its small size Anglo-Jewry was a divided community, consisting of two groups which had little contact with each other. The Sephardi Jews had been the original settlers, coming from Holland and tracing their roots back to the Spanish Peninsula. A high proportion of them were merchants and many were already integrated into European culture. The Askenazi Jews had arrived later from Central Europe. They were generally of the poorer classes and much more steeped in Jewish tradition. By the end of the 18th century they outnumbered the Sephardi Jews, although the latter continued to regard themselves as the aristocracy and tried to dissociate themselves from the newcomers.

19.2   1802 Sephardi and Askenazi Differences

'In processes of time the German Jews influenced by the benignity of this Government, resorted to this country, but the Spanish and Portuguese Jews and the German Jews always considered each other (as they actually are) separate and distinct bodies.

'First, because the charitable institutions formed by the Spanish and Portuguese Jews were solely directed to assist their brethren, who either fled from the alluded persecution, or were reduced by other misfortunes, and not for the purpose of encouraging German, Dutch, or Polish adventurers — and —

'Secondly, because in various ceremonies and customs the German Jews, differing much from the Portuguese, erected periodically various Synagogues in order to follow their own peculiar method. This, as well as the pronunciation of dialect of their Hebrew, so different from that of the Portuguese, and which rendered it impossible for them to read Prayers together, contributed to form of them two distinct (not Religious, but) political Bodies.

'In addition to the foregoing, it is necessary to observe, another cause now tends more than ever to make it the interest of the Spanish and Portuguese Jews to keep themselves a distinct body — namely, because not having increased in number, their establishments remain competent to their wants — whereas within the last fifty years the German Jews have increased prodigiously in number, coming from all parts of Germany, *and mostly of the poorer class*. So that their poor bears no proportion to the Portuguese poor, who have suitable establishments and are well provided for, while they have none and want for everything'.

Minutes of the Board of Deputies

Many of the Ashkenazi Jews suffered from dire poverty. At a time when there were no general welfare facilities, the full burden of the problem fell upon the Synagogues.

19.3   1801 The Poverty of Ashkenazi Jews

'The opulent are but few, and the middling class altho' not so few, possess but little, the bulk of the Nation which comprehends a very numerous poor. It is that demands my utmost consideration.

Many and incessant are the applications for assistance from

this class, on those who can any way afford to give it, but all that can be procured is never adequate to the present want, much less can it ward off the future; nor is there any prospect for the families bettering their state, since they have no regular trade whereby to earn a maintenance. The few means they follow, such as dealing in old cloaths &c. are daily becoming less productive, and at present they know no other.

The infirm, the lame, the blind, and the helpless aged, are compleatly wretched; since the Synagogue funds can afford them but a very scanty pittance, and they cannot take shelter in a Christian parish workhouse. The sick indeed are not quite destitute of medical aid, being looked to by the Synagogues appointment, or dispensarys, but what avails medicine where Nurses, Bedding, and even food are wanting?

The Synagogue administration with respect to the poors aid, is at least in the Metropolis very inadequate as to funds, and ill directed as to manner; nor is either evil easily remedied.

The funds in all these Synagogues are raised by the rent every person pays for his seat in that which he frequents, together with the offerings made on festivals and particular occasions, and as they have no direct means of enforcing payment, a great deal of this income is very uncertain.

These Synagogues are generally speaking independent of each other, and of course involve distinct interests; all their reliefs to the poor are dispensed in money at the discretion of the overseers with some limitation, excepting some stated and trifling stipends, fixed by the vestrys to a specific list, and a distribution of passover cakes during the week of that festival; they likewise defray the charges of burials.

It is very evident that this relief is far short of being even temporarily effectual, both from its inadequateness to the extent required, and from the vague manner of its dispensations; but the worst circumstance is, that the distresses must inevitably always recur, as these poor have scarce any method of procuring a maintanance. Every possible evil must hence ensue, and every meanness and vice that can debase the human character becomes the consequence of the degradation of mind induced by desponding poverty'.

Joshua van Oven

111

Fig. 38. The 'Rag Fair' in Rosemary Lane, Houndsditch

Many Ashkenazi Jews eked out a living as peddlers, selling buckles, buttons, sealing wax, oranges, lemons, pencils, necklaces and watches. Travelling to all parts of the country in search of trade, they often set up outposts which later became the basis for provincial Jewish communities. Their dominant trade, however, was old clothes.

19.4   1830 The Old Clothes Hawker

'The other day I was floored by a Jew. He passed me several times crying for old clothes in the most nasal and extraordinary tone I ever heard. At last I was so provoked, that I said to him, 'Pray, why can't you say "old clothes" in a plain way as I do now?' The Jew stopped, and looking very gravely at me, said in a clear and even fine accent, 'Sir, I can say "old clothes" as well you can; but if you had to say so ten times a minute for an hour together, you would say "*Ogh Clo*" as I do now'; and so he marched off. I was so confounded with the justice of his retort, that I followed and gave him a shilling, the only one I had'.

Samuel Taylor Coleridge

Fig. 39. Daniel Mendoza (left) in his successful fight against Richard Humphreys at Stilton 6th May 1789 to become champion boxer of England.

Whilst most Jewish children would receive education of some sort, the standard of tuition was poor. Voices began to be raised towards educational reform.

19.5   1818 Jewish Education

'Most of the instructors of the young depart from the proper path in the matter of reading and grammar. Before a child can read properly they teach him to translate the Pentateuch into [Judeo-] German. This plague has become generally prevalent, and it is like a spreading infection among our fellow-Jews, who foolishly call this language 'Jewish' and persist in regarding it as Holy. As for me, they raised their voices against me and called me a dangerous innovator, because I began to translate the Hebrew for my pupils into English, which they consider a base secular language. ... The purport of what I have said is to show my contemporaries that anyone who teaches in Great Britain has not done his duty with his tender pupils if he instructs them according to the method described above that has become established in our midst. He should first teach him to read Hebrew accurately, and then how to translate it into English; and he must not confuse his mind even with pure German or Spanish for all this labour is superfluous and useless. Hence, from as soon as the child can begin to speak, his father or teacher should teach him in the manner I have described'.

E. P. Marks *The Key to the Sacred Language*

19.6 **1780's Jewish Women**

I will now take a view of the Jewish Women, but to do that, I must for a time withdraw from the Synagogue, for *that* is *not* the place to find them, for they so seldom go to prayers. However, I am not going to condemn them on *that* account, the *fault* is *not* their own. The generality of them are *Foreigners*, from Germany, Poland, etc., where to read and write in their native tongue, is held highly *criminal*; hence they are prevented from associating with Christians, as well as from reading the *German* or *Polish* translations of the *Bible*. . . . The are brought up either under their own Parents or a Jewish Tutor. Who can teach them no *established language* whatever. For the tutors *themselves* speak but a kind of *Gibberish*, or fulsome compound of Hebrew, German and Dutch, which none but the *German Jews* are capable of understanding. . . . It is owing to this ignorance, that the Jewish Women so seldom go to Synagogue. . . .

A Peep into the Synagogue

It was commonly held — although never proven — that one of the conditions for the Readmission was that Jews should not proselytise. As a result even those wishing to convert to Judaism out of their own free will were discouraged by the religious authorities. The Scottish aristocrat, Lord George Gordon,

shocked both society and Anglo-Jewry by converting in Holland
and returning to England a Jew.

19.7   c.1787 The Ballad of Lord George Gordon

Ye Jews, Turks and Christians, I pray now draw near,
When a comical ditty you quickly will hear,
Concerning Lord George who for Protestant laws,
His life said he'd lose in so glorious a cause.
Derry down, etc.
In Seventeen hundred and eighty's fam'd year
At the head of the Protestants he did appear,
When prisons came down and houses did burn[1],
Who'd have thought that his Lordship a Smouchy[2] wou'd
    turn?
Then to Birmingham posted my Lord in a trice,
And because that his stomach it was very nice,
He swore that no pork or fat bacon he'd eat,
For the devil was conjur'd into that foul meat.
To a Jew he turn'd, with a beard long as a goat,
The Mosaical law he has now got by rote.
What a glorious defender of Protestant laws!
With pork or fat bacon I'd well rub his jaws.
A snoga[3] he promis's the Smouches to build,
With what glorious ideas his nob must be fill'd,
First a Protestant leader, the head of them all,
Now this Christian is turn'd and a Jew we him call.
So we wish them much joy of this new convert Jew,
Tho' my tale it is odd, yet I'm sure it is true,
So farewell my Lord, since to Newgate you're taken[4],
You may find it a hard case to save your own bacon.

The Christian Turned Jew

1. *He led the 'No Popery Riots' in London in 1780.*
2. *A slang term for a Jew.*
3. *A Sephardi term for a synagogue.*
4. *He was sentenced to two years imprisonment for libelling the Queen of France.*

Jews in 19th Century Literature

Until the 19th Century, the image of the Jew in English literature had largely been the conventional portrait of the Jew as a figure of mystery and terror. In Sir Walter Scott's novel, *Ivanhoe*, set in King John's England, Isaac of York is shown in a much more sympathetic light.

20.1 **1819 Ivanhoe**

'Can he afford a ransom?' answered the Prior. 'Is he not Isaac of York, rich enough to redeem the captivity of the ten tribes of Israel who were led into Assyrian bondage? ...

Marvel it is to all living Christian hearts that such gnawing adders should be suffered to eat into the bowels of the state, and even of the holy church herself, with foul usuries and extortions.'

'Hold, father,' said the Jew, 'mitigate and assuage your choler. I pray of your reverence to remember that I force my monies upon no one. But when churchman and layman, prince and prior, knight and priest, come knocking to Isaac's door, they borrow not his shekels with these uncivil terms. It is then, ''Friend Isaac, will you pleasure us in this matter, and our day shall be truly kept, so God sa'me?'' — and ''Kind Isaac, if ever you served man, show yourself a friend in this need!'' And when the day comes, and I ask my own, then what hear I but ''Damned Jew,'' and ''The curse of Egypt on your tribe,'' and all that may stir up the rude and uncivil populace against poor strangers!'

'Prior,' said the captain, 'Jew though he be, he hath in this spoke well. Do thou, therefore, name his ransom, as he named thine, without farther rude terms.'

When Ivanhoe is wounded, he is tended by Isaac's daughter, Rebecca:

20.2　'I will accomplish my promise,' said Rebecca, 'and thou shalt bear thine armour on the eighth day from hence, if thou wilt grant me but one boon in the stead of the silver thou dost promise me.'

'If it be within my power, and such as a true Christian knight may yield to one of thy people,' replied Ivanhoe, 'I will grant thy boon blythely and thankfully.'

'Nay,' answered Rebecca, 'I will but pray of thee to believe henceforward that a Jew may do good service to a Christian, without desiring other guerdon[1] than the blessing of the Great Father who made both Jew and Gentile.'

1. Reward

In poetry too, the new spirit of romance and humanitarianism influenced the presentation of the Jews. Wordsworth composed *The Jewish Family* and Lord Byron also wrote on their sufferings:

20.3　**1815 Hebrew Melodies**

Oh! weep for those that wept by Babel's stream,
Whose shrines are desolate, whose land a dream;
Weep for the harp of Judah's broken shell;
Mourn — where their God hath dwelt the godless dwell!
And where shall Israel lave her bleeding feet?
And when shall Zion's songs again seem sweet?
And Judah's melody once more rejoice
The hearts that leap'd before its heavenly voice?
Tribes of the wandering foot and weary breast,
How shall ye flee away and be at rest!
The wild-dove hath her nest, the fox his cave,
Mankind their country — Israel but the grave!

In the works of Charles Dickens, two portraits of the Jew were presented: the corrupting and miserly Fagin, and the amiable and generous Mr. Riah.

The Jew stepped gently to the door: which he fastened. He then drew forth: as it seemed to Oliver, from some trap in the floor: a small box, which he placed carefully on the table. His eyes glistened as he raised the lid, and looked in. Dragging an old chair to the table, he sat down; and took from it a magnificent gold watch, sparkling with jewels.

'Aha!' said the Jew, shrugging up his shoulders, and distorting every feature with a hideous grin. 'Clever dogs! Clever dogs! Staunch to the last! Never told the old parson where they were. Never peached upon old Fagin! And why should they? It wouldn't have loosened the knot, or kept the drop up, a minute longer. No, no, no! Fine fellows! Fine fellows!'

With these, and other muttered reflections of the like nature, the Jew once more deposited the watch in its place of safety. At least half a dozen more were severally drawn forth from the same box, and surveyed with equal pleasure; besides rings, brooches, bracelets, and other articles of jewellery ... and, leaning back in his chair, muttered:

'What a fine thing capital punishment is! Dead men never repent; dead men never bring awkward stories to light. Ah, it's a fine thing for the trade! Five of 'em strung up in a row, and none left to play booty, or turn white-livered!'

20. 5   **1863 Our Mutual Friend**

''For instance,'' (Fledgeby) resumed ... ''who but you and I ever heard of a poor Jew?''

''The Jews,'' said the old man (Riah), raising his eyes from the ground with his former smile. ''They hear of poor Jews often, and are very good to them.''

20.6   For it is not, in Christian countries, with the Jews as with other peoples. Men say, 'This is a bad Greek, but there are good Greeks. This is a bad Turk, but there are good Turks.' Not so with the Jews. Men find the bad among us easily enough — among what peoples are the bad not easily found? —

Fig. 40. The Jew and Morris both begin to understand each other.

Fig. 41. Mr. Riah converses with Miss Wren

119

but they take the worst of us as samples of the best; they take the lowest of us as presentations of the highest; and they say, 'All Jews are alike.'

Towards the end of the century, George Eliot not only treated individual Jewish characters favourably, but she also expounded on the nobility of the Jewish race as a whole:

20.7 **1876 Daniel Deronda**

''Well, whatever the Jews contributed at one time, they are a standstill people,'' said Lilly. ''They are the type of obstinate adherence to the superannuated. They may show good abilities when they take up liberal ideas, but as a race they have no development in them.''

''That is false!'' said Mordecai, leaning forward again with his former eagerness. ''Let their history be known and examined: let the seed be sifted, let its beginning be traced to the weed of the wilderness — the more glorious will be the energy that transformed it. Where else is there a nation of whom it may be as truly said that their religion and law and moral life mingled as the stream of blood in the heart and made one growth — where else a people who kept and enlarged their spiritual store at the very time when they were hunted with a hatred as fierce as the forest-fires that chase the wild beast from his covert? There is a fable of the Roman, that swimming to save his life he held the roll of his writings between his teeth and saved them from the waters. But how much more than that is true of our race? They struggled to keep their place among the nations like heroes — yea, when the hand was hacked off, they clung with the teeth; but when the plough and the harrow had passed over the last visible signs of their national covenant, and the fruitfulness of their land was stifled with the blood of the sowers and planters, they said, 'The spirit is alive, let us make it a lasting habitation — lasting because movable — so that it may be carried from generation to generation, and our sons unborn may be rich in the things that have been, and possess a hope built on an unchangeable foundation.' They said it and they wrought it, though often breathing with scant life, as in a coffin, or as lying wounded amid a heap of slain. Hooted

120

and scared like the unowned dog, the Hebrew made himself envied for his wealth and wisdom, and was bled of them to fill the bath of Gentile luxury; he absorbed knowledge, he diffused it; his dispersed race was a new Phoenicia working the mines of Greece and carrying their products to the world. The native spirit of our tradition was not to stand still, but to use records as a seed, and draw out the compressed virtues of law and prophecy; and while the Gentile, who had said, 'What is yours is ours, and no longer yours,' was reading the letter of our law as a dark inscription, or was turning its parchments into shoe-soles for an army rabid with lust and cruelty, our Masters were still enlarging and illuminating with fresh-fed interpretation. But the dispersion was wide, the yoke of oppression was a spiked torture as well as a load; the exile was forced afar among brutish people, where the consciousness of his race was no clearer to him than the light of the sun to our fathers in the Roman persecution, who had their hiding-place in a cave, and knew not that it was day save by the dimmer burning of their candles. What wonder that multitudes of our people are ignorant, narrow, superstitious? What wonder?''

20th century writers have been much less interested in the Jews than their 19th century predecessors — perhaps because Jews are now socially and politically accepted, and are no longer an issue in themselves. A new phenomenon has emerged however: the pro-liferation of Jewish authors and playwrights[1] writing, among other things, on Jewish themes and experiences in their own terms.

1. For a comprehensive list, see the signatories to the Sunday Times letter (text 24.4).

Background Reading:
Montagu Frank Modder The Jew in the Literature of England p.108-155, 217-236, 267-309.
Harold Fisch The Dual Image — A Study of the Jew in English Literature p.53-79.

21

The Great Immigration

When Czar Alexander II was assassinated by revolutionaries in 1881, the Russian government attempted to deflect popular discontent by launching an anti-semitic campaign. Jewish rights of trade and residence were restricted, and there were many officially-inspired pogroms. The Jews responded to the persecution with mass emigration; some three million Jews emigrated to the West between 1881 and 1914. The majority went to the United States; some 100,000 settled in England, making an enormous impact on the existing community of 60,000 Jews.

21.1   1889 Immigrants Arriving

Let us imagine ourselves on board a Hamburg boat steaming slowly up the Thames in the early hours of the morning. In the stern of the vessel we see a mixed crowd of men, women, and children — Polish and Russian Jews, some sitting on their baskets, others with bundles tied up in bright-coloured kerchiefs. For the most part they are men between twenty and forty years of age, of slight and stooping stature, of sallow and pinched countenance, with low foreheads, high cheek-bones and protruding lips. They wear uncouth and dirt-bespattered garments, they mutter to each other in a strange tongue. Scattered among them a few women (their shapely figures and soft skins compare favourably with the sickly appearance of the men), in peasant frocks with shawls thrown lightly over their heads; and here and there a child, with prematurely set features, bright eyes, and agile movements ...

The steamer is at rest, the captain awaits the visit of the Custom House officials. All eyes are strained, searching through the shifting mist and dense forest of masts for the first glimpse of the eagerly hoped-for relations and friends, for the first sight of the long-dreamt-of city of freedom and prosperity.

Presently a boat rows briskly to the side of the vessel; seated in it a young woman with mock sealskin coat, vandyke hat slashed up with blue satin, and surmounted with a yellow ostrich feather, and long six-buttoned gloves. She is chaffing the boatman in broken English, and shouts words of welcome and encouragement to the simple bewildered peasant who peers over the side of the vessel with two little ones clasped in either hand. Yes! that smartly dressed young lady is her daughter. Three years ago the father and the elder child left the quiet Polish village: a long interval of suspense, then a letter telling of an almost hopeless struggle, at last passage-money, and here today the daughter with her bright, warm clothes and cheery self-confidence — in a few hours the comfortably furnished home of a small wholesale orange-dealer in Mitre Street, near to Petticoat Lane.

Seated by the side of the young woman a bearded man, his face furrowed and shoulders bent with work. He is comfortably clothed and wears a large watch-chain hanging ostentatiously outside his coat. Evidently he is not the father of the girl, for his hands are clenched nervously as he fails to catch sight of the long-expected form; he is simply the presser from the sweater's next door to the orange-dealer; and he also can afford the 1s. fee to board the steamer and meet his wife. Ah! there she is! and a gentle-faced woman, beaming with heightened colour, pushes her way to the side of the vessel, holding up the youngest child with triumphant pride ...

The scenes at the landing-stage are less idyllic. There are a few relations and friends awaiting the arrival of the small boats filled with immigrants: but the crowd gathered in and about the gin-shop overlooking the narrow entrance of the landing-stage are dock loungers of the lowest type and professional 'runners'. These latter individuals, usually of the Hebrew race, are among the most repulsive of East London parasites; boat after boat touches the landing-stage, they push forward, seize hold of the bundles or baskets of the newcomers, offer bogus tickets to those who wish to travel forward to America, promise guidance and free lodging to those who hold in their hands addresses of acquaintances in Whitechapel, or who are absolutely friendless. A little man with an official badge

(Hebrew Ladies' Protective Society) fights valiantly in their midst for the conduct of unprotected females[1], and shouts or whispers to the others to go to the Poor Jews' Temporary Shelter in Leman Street. For a few moments it is a scene of indescribable confusion: cries and counter-cries; the hoarse laughter of the dock loungers at the strange garb and broken accent of the poverty-stricken foreigners; the rough swearing of the boatmen at passengers unable to pay the fee for landing. In another ten minutes eighty of the hundred newcomers are dispersed in the back slums of Whitechapel; in another few days, the majority of these, robbed of the little they possess, are turned out of the 'free lodgings' destitute and friendless.

Beatrice Potter in *Life and Labour of the People of London*

1. *Who were sometimes duped into prostitution or shipped to South America as slaves.*

Fig. 42. Aliens arriving at Irongate Stairs, a contemporary impression.

124

Almost 50% of the immigrants — male and female — went into the tailoring trade and the notorious "sweat-shops":

21.2   1888 Sweating

I determined to chance my luck, and closed[2] with a tailor who offered to teach me the trade and give me lodgings and coffee for three weeks, and six shillings a week afterwards, until I learned one branch of the trade (coat-making) when I would be able, he said, to demand from four to eight shillings a day for my toil. He lived in one of the many dirty streets in Spitalfields, and the work he made was railway and seamen's coats — hard heavy work, that required more brute strength than skill. He occupied two rooms on the second floor, for which he paid seven shillings a week; had a wife, and three children aged respectively seven, four, two; very intelligent, almost crafty.

The room we worked in was used for cooking also, and there I had to sleep on the floor. The wife helped as much as she could at the trade, besides doing all the work of the house and the children. A young woman worked the machine from eight in the morning till nine at night, for three shillings a day; not very often making a full week's work. My work at first was to keep up a good fire with coke, and soap the seams and edges; and the elbow grease I used was considerable. I had to get up in the morning about half past five, and we finished at night between ten and eleven, and turned out every week about thirty coats, which came to about four pounds. The master himself worked very hard indeed; and he himself told me afterwards that he had left the old country for the same reason as myself, and that a few years previously he had been a cowkeeper and dairyman, but was now a 'tailor'.[3]

Myer Wilchinski *History of a Sweater*

2. *Made an agreement with.*
3. *The boot, shoe and slipper trade was the next most common occupation for the immigrants, followed by the furniture trade.*

21.3   1888 A Sweater

... we had a lengthy conversation with the wife of a sweater, who was very unhappy because her husband had taken to sweating. It would have been better had he resisted the promptings of ambition and modestly contented himself with being sweated. Now, he had to pay the rent of a workshop, the cost of gas and of eight or nine machines; and he got gentlemen's coats to make, with six button-holes, for elevenpence. It was starvation for him and his workpeople; and, glancing round at the furniture and general condition of this sweater's home, it certainly looked like starvation.

The Lancet

Fig. 43. The Cheap Tailor and His Workmen. A contemporary cartoon of the East End sweatshops at the turn of the century.

Hardship and struggle characterised all aspects of life for the immigrants, although family closeness and a strong sense of community acted as a partial compensation.

21.4   Early 1900s Makeshift Furniture

Furniture? ... One orange box — it was covered with a nice piece of material. We had orange boxes for to eat on ... We had three chairs. My younger sister: a boy wanted to take her home, wanted to take her back, so she said, ''I can't bring a boy home. We've only got three legs on one chair, where's he gonna sit?''

Resident of the East End

21.5   Late 1890s Cramped Conditions

Living downstairs in the basement there was a family called Binstock. They had eleven children, including two sets of twins. When it was hot in the summer the husband and wife used to sit on chairs out in the playground, because they couldn't sleep with all that crowd of children. It was hot — and perhaps buggy — and so they slept in the playground.

Resident of the East End

21.6   Early 1900s Rent Problems

My mother used to go into her (a neighbour) every Monday to borrow rent, 5s. rent. And my mother used to give her — when she got to the Board of Guardians, Thursday — give it to her back ... And Monday it started again.

Resident of the East End

21.7   Late 1890s Good Neighbours

We had a Mrs Morris living in Rothschild Buildings at the time when I was there — I was friendly with the children. She had seven children. This Mrs Morris got on to a chair to put 1d. in the slot for her gas to go on, and she fell and broke her leg. Oh, tragedy! She was taken to the London Hospital. What should she do with her seven children? Well, it was no problem. All the neighbours collected around and said they'd take it in turns each day. One would go in the mornings to give them their breakfast to see that they'd get off to school, and in the evening when the husband comes home he'll take in the pot of whatever it was and they'll all feed together. And this went on until Mrs Morris came home. Now, on the day that she came home from the hospital, the neighbours all around collected together and washed the children, made them all clean, sat them in a row. There was a baby there, tied to a chair with a towel so he couldn't wriggle out. When her husband brought Mrs Morris home from the hospital she was so overwhelmed by this party, they'd collected some cakes and things and made it all look very nice, that she burst out crying. It was really wonderful to know that her family were being taken care of by her neighbours.

Resident of the East End

21.8   1903 Doctor's Verdict

When I came to examine the death rates, which I had expected to find very high in view of the conditions of the houses and the prevailing conditions of the district, I found them very low. I was very much interested to learn how it was that people who were living in close courts and crowded alleys under conditions which I was accustomed to find associated with high death rates wherever I looked in London, had a low death rate ... In the end the only conclusion I could come to was that the difference in the death rate was due to the better care the inhabitants took of themselves and their mode of life.

The Royal Commission on Alien Immigration

Fig. 44. Providence Place in the East End 1905

Many of the immigrants brought with them their deep attachment to Judaism and soon established scores of small Synagogues or 'shtiebls':

21.9   **1889 The Shtiebl**

Here, early in the morning, or late at night, the devout members meet to recite the morning and evening prayers, or to decipher the sacred books of the Talmud. And it is a curious and touching sight to enter one of the poorer and more wretched of these places on a Sabbath morning. Probably the one you choose will be situated in a small alley or narrow court, or it may be built out in a back-yard. To reach the entrance you stumble over broken pavement and household debris; possibly you pick your way over the rickety bridge connecting it with the cottage property fronting the street. From the outside it appears a long wooden building surmounted by a skylight, very similar to the ordinary sweater's workshop.

... the heat and odour convince you that the skylight is not used for ventilation. From behind the trellis of the 'ladies gallery' you see at the far end of the room the richly curtained Ark of the Covenant, wherein are laid, attired in gorgeous vestments, the sacred scrolls of the Law. Slightly elevated on a platform in the midst of the congregation stands the reader or minister, surrounded by the seven who are called up to the reading of the Law from among the congregation. At last you step out, stifled by the heat and dazed by the strange contrast of the old-world memories of a majestic religion and the squalid vulgarity of an East End slum.

... if you could follow the quick spoken Judisch, you would be still more bewildered by these 'destitute foreigners' ... the men are scattered over the benches (maybe there are several who are still muttering their prayers), or they are gathered together in knots, sharpening their intellects with the ingenious points and subtle logic of the Talmudical argument, refreshing their minds from the rich stores of Talmudical wit, or listening with ready helpfulness to the tale of distress of a newcomer from the foreign home.

Beatrice Potter in *Life and Labour of the People of London*

21.10 Early 1900s Sabbath Fires

'My mother was very orthodox and we never lit a fire on
Saturday. So we used to get a youngster in on Friday night,
after the Sabbath was in, to put more coal on the fire. And then
the fire would go out and she'd come on a Saturday morning
and light it, and come during the day to put more coal on, and
at the end of the day she'd come along and you'd give her a
couple of coppers. These kids were around, you know, and
they'd come week after week. They might have been 10 or 11,
12, something like that.'

Resident of the East End

While many Jews worked to aid the new immigrants, others
were worried by the effect of the sudden influx, and the Chief
Rabbi asked East European Rabbis to try to stem the tide:

21.11 1888 Chief Rabbi Intervenes

...it is difficult for them to support themselves and their
households, and at times they contravene the will of their
Maker on account of poverty and over-work, and violate the
Sabbath and Festivals. Some have been ensnared in the net of
the missionaries and renounced their religion, may the Merciful
save.

There are many who believe that all the cobblestones of
London are precious stones, and that it is the place of gold.
Woe and alas, it is not so ...

I implore every rabbi of a community kindly to preach in the
synagogue and house of study, to publicize the evil which is
befalling our brethren who have come here, and to warn them
not to come to the land of Britain for such ascent is a descent.

Nathan Marcus Adler in *HaMeliz*

In some quarters there was a hostile reaction to the immigrants:

21.12 1892 The Alien Invasion

When visiting the poor when times were bad I often heard

the weary complaint, 'It's them Jews'. Time after time I heard that lament. Many men and women, struggling to keep a home over their heads, but driven out of work by the foreigner, who could 'live on less', and would take less, and work longer, have said to me, 'What's the use? The Jews are coming by thousands, and there will be nothing left.'

Rev. G. S. Reaney in *The Destitute Alien in Great Britain*

21.13 1903 Jews Are Different

The aliens will not conform to our ideas, and, above all, they have no sort of neighbourly feeling ... A foreign Jew will take a house, and he moves in on a Sunday morning, which rather, of course, upsets all the British people there. Then his habits are different. You will see the houses with sand put down in the passages instead of oilcloth or carpet. These are little things, but they all serve to make a difference.

J. L. Silver in *Royal Commission on Alien Immigration*

Public pressure led to the establishment of a Royal Commission on the immigration of aliens. It culminated in the Aliens Act, which tightened entry regulations, although maintaining the right of asylum from persecution.

21.14 1905 The Aliens Act

An immigrant shall be considered an undesirable immigrant

(a) if he cannot show that he has in his possession, or is in a position to obtain, the means of decently supporting himself and his dependants (if any);

(b) if he is a lunatic or idiot, or owing to disease or infirmity appears likely to become a charge upon the rates or otherwise a detriment to the public;

(c) if he has been sentenced in a foreign country with which there is an extradition treaty for a crime, not being an offence of a political character, which is as respects that country, an extradition crime within the meaning of the Extradition Act, 1870;

(d) if an expulsion order under this Act has been made in his case; but in the case of an immigrant who proves that he is seeking admission to this country solely to avoid persecution or punishment on religious or political grounds, or for an offence of a political character, or persecution, involving danger of imprisonment or danger to life and limb, on account of religious belief, leave to land shall not be refused on the ground merely of want of means ...

Commenting on the Act, the then Prime Minister said:

21.15   1905 Jewish Separatism

"A state of things could easily be imagined in which it would not be to the advantage of the civilization of the country that there should be an immense body of persons who, however patriotic, able and industrious — however much they threw themselves into the national life — still by their own action remained a people apart and not merely held a religion differing from the vast majority of their fellow countrymen, but only intermarried among themselves".

Arthur Balfour

The Aliens Act did not halt the flow of immigration which continued in large numbers till 1914.

A driving ambition to better themselves socially and economically characterized many of the immigrants.

21.16   1889 The 'Greeners' Settle

If we were able to follow the 'greener'[4] into the next scene of his adventures we should find him existing on the charity of a co-religionist or toiling day and night for a small labour-contractor in return for a shake-down, a cup of black coffee, and a hunch of brown bread. This state of dependence, however, does not last. For a time the man works as if he were a slave under the lash, silently, without complaint. But in a few months (in the busy season in a few weeks) the master enters his workshop and the man is not at his place. He has left without warning — silently — as he worked without pay. He

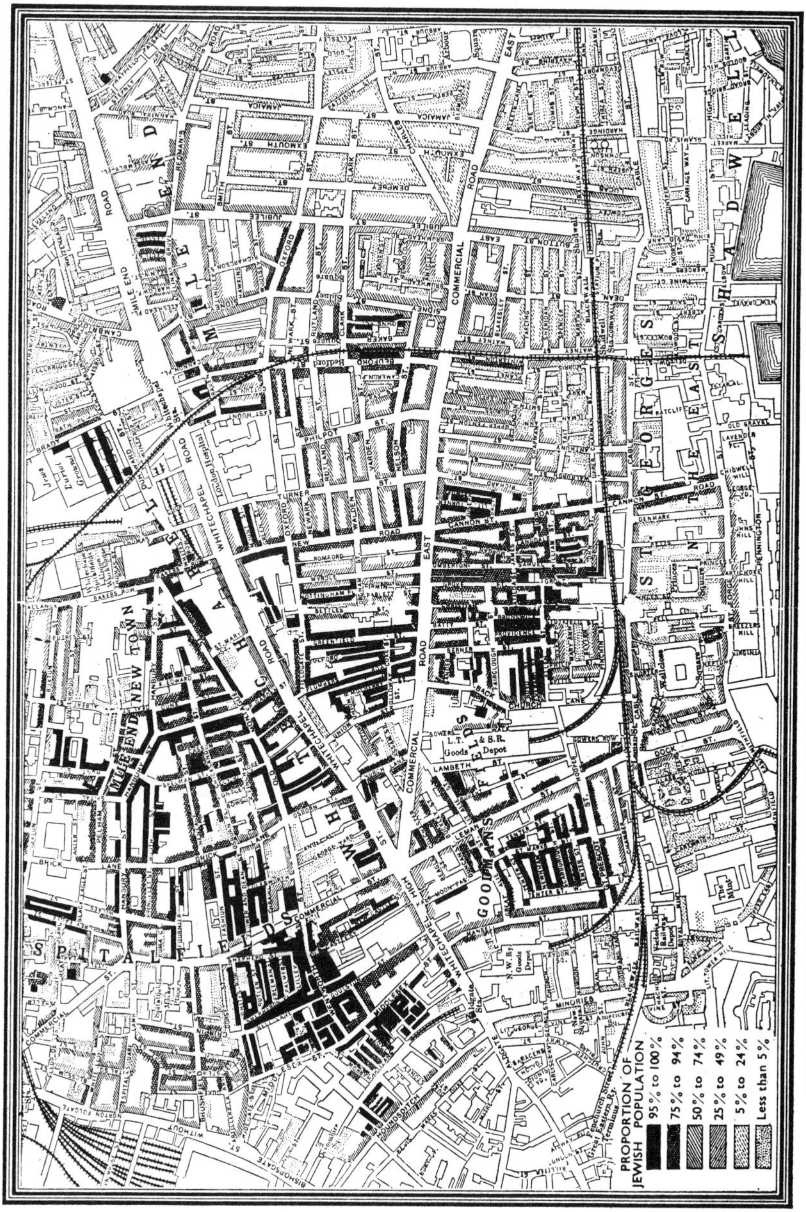

THE EAST END OF LONDON c. 1900, SHOWING JEWISH RESIDENTS IN PROPORTION TO THE TOTAL POPULATION

(Adapted from Russell and Lewis, *The Jew in London*).

N.B.   The Mile End area shown in the upper right-hand part of the Map is that referred to in the text as Mile End Old Town.

PROPORTION OF
JEWISH POPULATION

95% to 100%
75% to 94%
50% to 74%
25% to 49%
5% to 24%
Less than 5%

Fig. 45. The Jewish East End 1900

133

has learnt his trade and can sell his skill in the open market at the corner of Commercial Street; or possibly a neighbouring sweater, pressed with work, has offered him better terms. A year hence he has joined a Chevras[5], or has become a habitué of a gambling club. And unless he falls a victim to the Jewish passion for gambling, he employs the enforced leisure of the slack season in some form of petty dealing. He is soon in a fair way to become a tiny capitalist — a maker of profit as well as an earner of wage. He has moved out of the back court in which his fellow-countrymen are herded together like animals, and is comfortably installed in a model dwelling; the walls of his parlour are decked with prints of Hebrew worthies, or with portraits of prize-fighters and race-horses; his wife wears jewellery and furs on the Sabbath; for their Sunday dinner they eat poultry. He treats his wife with courtesy and tenderness, and they discuss constantly the future of the children. He is never to be seen at the public-house round the corner; but he enjoys a quiet glass of 'rum and shrub' and a game of cards with a few friends on the Saturday or Sunday evening; and he thinks seriously of season tickets for the People's Palace. He remembers the starvation fare and the long hours of his first place: he remembers, too, the name and address of the wholesale house served by his first master; and presently he appears at the counter and offers to take the work at a lower figure, or secures it through a tip to the foreman. But he no longer kisses the hand of Singer's agent and begs with fawning words for another sewing machine; neither does he flit to other lodgings in the dead of night at the first threat of the broker. In short, he has become a law-abiding and self-respecting citizen of our great metropolis, and feels himself the equal of a Montefiore or a Rothschild.[6]

Beatrice Potter in *Life and Labour of the People of London*

4. *A new immigrant in search of work.*
5. *Small Synagogues with their own friendly society covering bereavement benefits.*
6. *The process of self-improvement often continued with each generation; thus the father might be a tailor, the son a businessman, and the grandson a doctor.*

Fig. 46. The Cheepers, Jewish immigrant family, 1911.

Background Reading:

Chaim Bermant *Point of Arrival* p.122-163.

V. D. Lipman *Social History of the Jews in England 1850-1950* p.85-133.

Lloyd P. Gartner *The Jewish Immigrant in England 1870-1914.*

135

Provincial Communities

Today the Jewish community in Manchester is the second largest Jewish centre in Britain, but it had comparatively late origins. It started in the mid 18th century when itinerant hawkers from London began to settle in the town. One such hawker was Isaac Soloman who was attacked on the road between Manchester and Rochdale.

22.1 1740 Manchester Jew Robbed

'He was waylaid by two Men on Foot . . . the one a Low Broad-set Man, wearing a whitish caped Close Coat, and a brown Bob Wig; the other a tall thin Man, of pale complexion, wearing a Drab-colour'd Coat, white Metal Buttons, Blue Waistcoat, Check'd Shirt, and dark colour'd Hair who relieved him (according to his own account) of Nine Guineas, one Portugese Piece Value Three Pounds Twelve Shillings, Three Moidores Value Four Pounds One Shilling, One Half Guinea, and Ten Shillings in Silver; and the Goods hereafter mentioned, being of the value of Ten Pounds and upwards, viz two Pair of carved Silver Shoe Buckles, two Pairs of Silver Tea Tongs, one Pinchbeck Watch Chain, four Gold Rings, one Pinchbeck Head for a Cane, ten Pair of Chrystal Buttons, a Silver Watch Chain, three Silver Stock Buckles, one large Silver Clasp, a silver carved snuff-box, several pair of white Metal Buckles, several Japan Snuff-Boxes and Silver Thimbles.'

London Gazette

The Jewish population of Leeds — which is the highest proportion in the country — arose as a result of the mass influx of East European Jews at the end of the 19th century. The Jewish workers were highly organised and the first ever strike occurred

Fig. 47. Cheetham Hill Spanish and Portuguese Synagogue Built in 1873 it now serves as a Jewish Museum.

there in 1855. Sir Montague Burton introduced factory techniques that changed tailoring from a sweated trade to a mass production industry, while his chain of 'off-the-peg' shops was among the first to cater for the new mass-markets.

Despite being a relatively small Jewish community, Sunderland is one of many fiercely independent Jewish communities who make great efforts to build a communal infrastructure and maintain a Jewish life, with its own Board of Guardians, Jewish day-school, yeshiva (Rabbinic school), mikveh (ritual bath), kosher meat facilities, and two synagogues. It was also keen to play its part in the affairs of the nation.

22.2   1914 Serving The Country

'A largely attended meeting of members of the Hebrew congregation and their ladies was held in the Synagogue

Fig. 48. Clothing manufacture in the No. 2 Coat Room, Hudson Road Mills, Leeds of Montague Burton Ltd.

Today's 'Marks and Spencers' also originated in Leeds.

Fig. 49. Marks' Penny Bazaar, an impression of the first stall in Leeds 1884.

schoolrooms, Lawrence Street, yesterday afternoon for the purpose of devising the best ways and means of rendering help at this crisis. Mr. B. Jacoby, President of the Congregation, presided. ... The following Jewish furniture dealers have offered to supply beds and equipment for the beds: Messrs. B. Jacoby, Israel Jacobs, H. Berg, S. Gillis, D. Jockelson, I. Behrman, Coun. N. Richardson, E. Jacobs, I. Levy, D. Goldman, and H. Havelock. It was decided to establish a Jewish Women's Sewing Guild to supply garments and other necessaries for the sick and wounded, and a small committee was appointed, with Mrs. Isaac Behrman as Secretary, who will call a meeting at the earliest possible opportunity.

'Sixteen young Jews from Sunderland have joined the colours, and more are expected to join.'

Sunderland Echo

Fig. 50. Pages of the Milah (circumcision) Register, Sunderland

In the larger Jewish centres – such as Manchester, Leeds, Liverpool, Glasgow, Cardiff, Birmingham, Bournemouth, Brighton and Sheffield — representative councils have been established to co-ordinate the variety of different synagogues, cultural societies and welfare institutions.

22.3 1913 Formation of a Representative Council

'A Meeting of representatives of various institutions of the City met on Sunday, 14th inst. to consider a proposal to establish a permanent Central Council for the purpose of safe-guarding and protecting the interests of the Jewish Com-munity in Glasgow, to deal with any question, local or otherwise, not capable of being dealt with by any one individ-ual institution. ...

It is proposed that, for the Constitution of the Council, the various institutions be represented according to a scheme of proportional representation.'

Communal Circular

Scottish Jewry largely owes its origins to the two waves of immigrants in the 1880's and in the 1930's. Although mainly based in Glasgow, smaller communities are to be found in Edinburgh, Aberdeen and Dundee. Their experiences parallelled that of the immigrant Jews south of the border:

22.4 1939 Refugees' Experiences

'When the war broke out, I was still working in Edinburgh. Then the lady came and said, 'You are Hitler!' At first, I didn't know what she wanted. I didn't know that war had been declared. Then she said: 'war.' I had to look up the dictionary to find out what 'war' is. Then, for example, my son, who was at school, came home with a torn overcoat. I asked him: "What happened to you?" "Well, I got a big hitting. The boy thought, I am German, but I told him I'm Polish." I said: "You're not Polish." But what could I do. He said, "I think it is better, I tell them I am Polish."

Questions such as what had all this been about, you know,

Hitler coming to power and the war breaking and where was all this leading and what was going to happen and in those days socialism certainly seemed a way out of all these difficulties and so our activities at the centre and the cultural activities were geared towards widening our knowledge about what that really meant and we had some marvellous programmes. We participated in a young group of actors and we participated in a choir and when the War broke out we went right up to the north of Scotland where we took songs from Czechoslavakia, songs from the Spanish War, from Germany and then we had *Sprechchöre* but we didn't only do, that we wanted to let the Scots know how much we appreciated living here. We recited Burns at them with rather strange accents and they bore with us with a great deal of pleasure and even more tolerance.'

Interviews with refugees

Fig. 51. Regular advertisement for John Begg whisky in The Jewish Echo.

—— GLASGOW JEWISH ——
NATURALISATION SOCIETY
Founded by the Dr. Herzl Lodge No.12
of the Grand Order of Israel
A CALL
TO THE GLASGOW PUBLIC

Remember you are strangers in a strange land. You may live here for years, but if you are not naturalised you remain strangers. Therefore see to it that you don't miss the opportunity that you have now.

Now, when foreigners have so many difficulties in this country, it is very important for all Jews to take advantage of the privilege to become English subjects.

YOU CAN PAY FOR THIS AT 1 SHILLING PER WEEK.

Don't hold back from this. A Jew must have a home; a home is very dear; therefore become English citizens.

BECOME NATURALISED!
All particulars are available from our Secretary:
Mr. B. Glasser, 108 South Portland Street.

Fig. 52. Advertisement 1921.

141

Gateshead is renowned for being one of the few communities that is solidly ultra-orthodox and whose existence is based around its famous Yeshiva (Rabbicical school).

Fig. 53. Gateshead Yeshiva.

Fig. 54. The Princes Road Synagogue, Liverpool, opened in 1875 was the first to introduce sermons preached in English.

23

Communal Organisations

In the 19th century, Anglo-Jewry was a tightly organised community, with committees and institutions covering all aspects of life. Welfare work had always been considered of paramount importance, motivated by both a concern for fellow Jews in difficulty and a desire to prevent the Jewish poor from becoming a public nuisance. The many charities were supported by the philanthropy of private individuals.

23.1 1898 A Successful Report

A meeting of the Committee of the East London Branch of the Home and Hospital for Jewish Incurables was held at the "Three Nuns" Hotel, Aldgate, on Thursday week, Mr. L. Schneiders in the chair.

Upon the proposition of Mr. Ralph Lazarus, a sum of fifty guineas was voted to the parent Institution.

Mr. Stuart M. Samuel stated that as President of the Home he considered it very advantageous that a large and influential Committee should be working on its behalf in East London. The results had been highly satisfactory. Their Honorary Secretary, Mr. Albert London, had just reported that between £800 and £900 had been placed on deposit to the credit of the Building Fund, in addition to an amount of one hundred guineas received in one year from annual subscriptions, and which they had so kindly already handed to the Treasurers of the Institution towards its maintenance. If the last Annual Report were consulted it would be found that this Branch had succeeded in obtaining over 300 subscribers. This result was most gratifying and one upon which the members of the East London Committee were to be congratulated. He took the opportunity of mentioning that the Board of Management upon the unanimous recommendation of the Ladies' and House

Committees, had determined to remove the patients from their present inadequate premises pending the erection of the new Home at Tottenham. Negotiations were proceeding to acquire a mansion known as The Berthons, situated at Wood Street, Walthamstow, and he trusted that with the generous assistance of the community sufficient annual funds would be provided to enable the Institution to receive some of the numerous applicants for admission. Mr. Samuel concluded by expressing his willingness to afford personal co-operation either in augmenting the number of workers on the Committee, or in a house to house canvass for additional subscribers.

The Jewish Chronicle

23.2 **1898 A New Building**

Jewish Association for the Protection of Girls and Women.

We have been requested to acquaint our readers, through the medium of this paper, that Mr. Joseph Pyke has purchased a valuable freehold property in Great Prescot Street, Aldgate, upon which he intends to erect a commodious building, in lieu of the present Lodging House for Respectable Jewish Girls, situated in Great Tenter Street, under the auspices of the Jewish Association for the Protection of Girls and Women.

This new building will bear the name, as indeed the present one does, of "Sara Pyke House", in memory of the late Mrs. Joseph Pyke, and it will be the generous gift of Mr. Pyke to the Association.

From its position, within easy walking distances of the Docks and the Aldgate Station, it will be admirably fitted for its purpose, and when completed will form an important addition to the many buildings that owe their existence to Jewish benevolence.

It is needless to say that the ladies who are interested in the work of the Association feel deeply grateful to the kind and thoughtful donor.

The Jewish Chronicle

1898 A Rousing Speech

The annual distribution of prizes to the inmates of the Jews' Hospital and Orphan Asylum was held on Sunday at the institution, West Norwood, and was attended by a large number of visitors, mostly relatives of the children.

Sir George Faudel-Phillips delivered a short address. He reminded the children that the institution was their second home; and that those who devoted so much thought and attention to their interests were their parents for the time being. But although Norwood was their home, they must not forget that England was their nation. They should take one of the numerous roads which England offered them, and should ever remember that they were English men and English women. When the time came for them to go forth into the world, he would like them to do what they took in hand thoroughly well and with determination. The members of the Committee were men who had more past than future. The children had a great deal more future than past, and he begged them to make good use of what lay between — the present. His own interest in the institution commenced when he was very young. He remembered his uncle, Mr. Henry Faudel, taking him over the Jews' Hospital when he was only six years of age. Since then the institution had grown in size and in reputation. It was a credit to their race and an example to any similar institution in England. It was as he had said, an old friend of his, and very dear to his heart, and it would grieve him very much to hear of a child who had left Norwood without following a good career and to the best of his or her ability. He begged them all, not only out of affection and gratitude for those who managed the institution, but in their own interest and that of their families and belongings, as well as of this great country, to do their best, always having a tender little spot in their hearts for the institution. — (Cheers).

The Jewish Chronicle

The Board of Guardians for the Relief of the Jewish Poor was founded in 1859 and assisted with a variety of needs. It became a model for the planners of the Welfare State and is now known as the Jewish Welfare Board.

The monthly meeting of the Jewish Board of Guardians was held on Monday at the offices, Middlesex Street. There were present: Mr. Benjamin L. Cohen, M.P., President, in the chair; Messrs. J. M. Ansell, A. E. Franklin, M. A. Green, Jacob Levy, E. J. Loewé, F. A. Lucas, Louis Samuel Montagu, Asher I. Myers, Charles Samuel and I. Seligman.

... The President urged on the members of the Board the imperative and urgent necessity of coming to the aid of the Institution before going on their holidays. He did not see his way to getting through the winter without generous support, especially as certain works which had to be done on the building would be a severe strain on the funds.

This appeal met with an immediate response, Mr. I. Seligman sending a slip to the President containing the words: "Your appeal has moved me to the extent of £50."

The meeting then terminated with a vote of thanks to the Chair.

The Jewish Chronicle

Fig. 55. Immigrants at the Jews Temporary Shelter in the East End of London, 1893.

The first Jewish Day School had been established in 1664, but the largest and most influential was the Jews' Free School, opened in 1817. There were no publicly-supported non-denominational schools at that time.

23.5   **1898 Early Memories of the Jews' Free School**

The opening of the important extension of the Jews' Free School — to be known as the Rothschild Wing — has suggested to us that our readers will be much interested in some early recollections of the Institution by old pupils. We give the premier publication to the reminiscences of one who is probably the oldest of Old Free School Boys now living —

Professor Marks

My recollections of the Jews' Free School extend back to 77 years ago, for I entered that Institution in the summer of 1821. The circumstances under which this happened were as follows: My father died in the July of that year, and this led to my being admitted into an Orphan Aid Society, directed by a Mr. Moses Daniel, a Mr. Philip Lazarus, and Rabbi Chanoch (father of the late Isaac Myers). This Society was in the habit of sending their beneficiaries to the Jews' Free School to receive their general education, and thus it came about that I was drafted into that Institution.

At the period of which I am speaking the Free School was situated in Ebenezer Square. Ebenezer Square was little better than a den in those days, it was entirely shut out from the genial influences of the sun's rays. As for the school itself, it consisted of little more than 100 boys. Not that the community were not equal to furnishing a very much larger number, but it was found exceedingly difficult to induce parents among the poorer classes to send their children to school. Boys of tender age were sent into the streets of London to earn a living by hawking pencils, cheap jewellery and fruit, and there were no public officials in those days to compel their attendance at school.

The instruction given in the Jews' Free School in these early days was of the lowest possible type. It consisted simply of English reading, spelling, and writing, the bare elements of

Hebrew reading, and the first four rules of arithmetic.

The Jewish Chronicle

Fig. 56. A lesson in home economics at the Jews Free School, London, 1902.

Organisations for young people were considered particularly vital, not just to occupy their spare time constructively, but also to instil English virtues of discipline and duty:

23.6 **1898 A Day in the Country with a Company of the Jewish Lads' Brigade.**

On Sunday last the residents of Whitechapel were roused by sounds of bugles and drums, and the martial tread of some 150 feet. It was the occasion of the annual inspection of the Brady Street Company of the Jewish Lads' Brigade. The lads mustered under Lieutenants M. E. Mosely and H. F. Phillips to the number of 71, there only being six absentees at the headquarters of the Company, the Brady Street Club for Working Boys, and were marched to London Bridge Station, where, after some difficulty, they were safely entrained for Mitcham. They were met at Mitcham Station by their Captain, Captain E. A. Myer, who then took command, and after a march through the quaint village, the parade ground (part of the grounds belonging to the residence where the Captain of the Company is now staying) was reached.

In the unavoidable and much-regretted absence of Colonel Goldsmid, who had intended being present, the lads were inspected by Colonel R. G. Grene, V.D., of the 2nd London V.R.C. On the Colonel arriving on the parade ground he was received with a general salute. A careful and minute inspection followed, after which the lads marched past in a very creditable style and were then put through several military evolutions by their Captain, the manual exercise being particularly good. At the conclusion of the drill, Colonel Grene addressed a few words to the lads. He expressed himself as being highly satisfied with the smart appearance and efficiency of the Company, which compared favourably with those of the Church Lads' Brigade, of which he had himself fifteen under his command. He wished to impress upon them the importance of discipline, which inculcates, as a direct result, the habits of cleanliness, self-respect and thoroughness in their work in after life. The Colonel concluded by commending the performance of the Bugle Band, which had only been in existence about three months. The Colonel was accompanied by Captain A. Lesser, the Brigade Transport Officer, who, addressing the lads, remarked on the great honour conferred on them by the presence of Colonel Grene.

The day's outing concluded with a cricket match followed by sports, the prizes for which were presented to the winners by Mrs. Henry Nathan.

A very substantial tea followed, the lads rivalling in this direction their performance in the earlier part of the afternoon. They were then marched back to the station, reaching London Bridge about nine, after spending a thoroughly enjoyable day.

The entire expense of the day's outing was borne by Mrs. Henry Nathan, for whom the boys gave three hearty cheers before leaving.

One interesting fact remains to be noted, showing the varied advantages of the Brigade. Whilst on the journey back to town a gentleman in the train fell into a fit. The train was stopped, and a messenger was sent to the boys' compartment to know if there were any ambulance boys among them. Sergeant A. Goldwater (a lad of nearly 15), immediately gave every assistance, and by the time the train reached town the gentleman had quite recovered.

In these ways the moral, physical and mental welfare of our East End lads is now being cared for. It is hoped that the public will recognise the advantages to be derived by the community from this movement, and will not withhold from its workers their moral and financial support.

The Jewish Chronicle

23.7 **1930 The Bernhard Baron St. George's Jewish Settlement**

At four o'clock there is a wave of excitement as the Play Centre doors are opened and the children stream in from school. The eager cries of those on the slides and swings mingle with the clamour of the percussion band and the thumping of pianos. Six o'clock comes and the stairs are momentarily blocked by a host of little girls in ballet skirts on the way to the "Rink". The clatter of small boys' boots resounds through the building as they make for the changing rooms. At 6.30 p.m. the adults in charge slip away to the restaurant for a hurried supper before the main stream of boys and girls pours in through the door. From then until ten o'clock every corner of the building is filled with life. Pianos and gramophones, cornets and saxophones, accordions and vocalists compete with the thumping of boxers, the shouts of those engaged in indoor games, the orderly behaviour of a discussion group and the impassioned oratory of amateur actors. Squash racquets, badminton racquets, handsaws, skipping ropes, cups and saucers, rubber-soled shoes, all add their accompaniment to the strange harmony of discordant sounds. At ten o'clock the clamour subsides, groups come together for their evening assemblies, heads are bowed in prayer. The solemn strains of Adon Olam flow in soft voices from the Girls' Club. Then the stairs become choked once more with throngs of happy people on their way home. In a few hours, the Settlement will be awakening to a new day.

Most of the Jewish organisations were founded by the Jewish upper and middle classes on behalf of the Jewish lower classes. The Jewish Trade Unions, however, were established by the workers themselves, often to the dismay of the Jewish leadership, who feared Socialism would lead to discontent and to atheism.

23.8 **1887 Rules of the Hebrew Cabinet Makers Association**

1. That this Association shall be called the "Hebrew Cabinet Makers' Association", and its Meetings be held at 69 Brick Lane, Spitalfields, in the County of Middlesex, on Saturday Evenings, at 8 o'clock, or any other time or place the Members may determine.

2. The object of this Association is to raise, by Contributions among its Members, a fund for the Protection of its Members, to assist them in obtaining a just price for their labour, to support its Members when out of Employment, or in Sickness, the payment of a sum of money on the death of a Member or Member's Wife, or the Insurance of Member's Tools: and to regulate the relations between workman and employer, and between workman and workman. And it shall consist of Journeymen Cabinet Makers and Carvers in all Branches of the Trade.

9. Should any Member knowingly take a job at a lower price than that fixed by the Members working in the same shop, accept, or offer to accept, or go to work in a shop where the men have been withdrawn by the advice of the Committee, on its being fully proved, he shall be fined such sum not exceeding 10s., or excluded, as the Members at the next Meeting shall decide on; subject to an appeal to summoned Meeting.

Should any person, not a Member, obtain employment where one or more Members are employed, it shall be the duty of such Member or Members to invite him to join the Association, and in case of refusal, they shall report the same to the Secretary, and continue so to do once a month.

31. Should any Free-Member be out of employment, he shall be entitled to 10s per week for six weeks, when no further benefit will be allowed until the expiration of eight weeks; if out of employment then, he shall be entitled to 10s. per week for six more weeks; but in no case to receive more than £6 in one year, nor less than three days' pay.

37. That any Member under 35 years of age by the payment

of 2d. per week: over 35 and under 50 years, 3d. per week, shall be entitled to 10s. in sickness per week for 12 weeks; such Member must have belonged to this benefit for six months, and paid Contributions for that time. Any Member joining this benefit will have to sign the form of declaration in Rule 36.

46. That on the decease of a Member who has been in the Association twelve months, his widow, nominee, or other person entitled, on producing a medical certificate as to the cause of death, shall be entitled to the sum of £2. 10s., and 10s. per year for each additional year he has been a Member of this Association, up to 5 years, the sum not to exceed £4. 10s.

56. Should a fire occur at any shop in the Trade where there are Members (and such Member free) lose their tools, they shall receive £2 compensation from the Association.

Fig. 57. Banner of the London Jewish Bakers' Union

The Jewish press brought together all the various activities within Anglo-Jewry, and gave it a strong sense of communal identity and direction. The oldest and most prominent publication is "The Jewish Chronicle".

1841 A New Arrival

דבר בעתו מה טוב משלי טו' כג'   "A word in its season how good it is." Proverbs, chap. 15, ver. 23.

No. 1.]   כח' מרחשון תרב' לפק'   NOVEMBER 12th, 5602.—1841.   [PRICE 2d.

TO OUR READERS.

We have always anticipated the appearance of a truly Jewish paper, with the most lively satisfaction; for we knew, that the existence among us, of an organ of mutual communication, was a desideratum of such magnitude, that the person supplying it would be entitled to the thanks of his brethren, and be a man to be envied. Our sentiments, therefore, on this occasion, when we ourselves are enabled to lay before you the required medium, are of the most grateful kind. We feel that we have done a something that may rescue us from the common fate of mankind—oblivion;—that we have projected (and it remains with you to say, whether our intentions shall be carried out to their fullest extent) a work, which, while it will make every Jew familiar with the condition of his fellow Israelites, will also supply him with the means of becoming better satisfied with his own, by teaching him how to render it subservient to a better lot; one that alone can secure happiness here, and ensure beatitude hereafter:—for with God's blessing, we would instruct him how to love mankind, and to seek his Creator.

We enter on our task then with alacrity, cheered to our prospective midnight labour and unceasing mental toil, by the bright, the glorious thought, that we may, under Divine Providence, be the humble instruments of regenerating, at least, a portion of our brethren; and like the " orb of night," while dispensing a gentle light to those may before you the required medium, rejoice in our own heaven-borrowed brilliancy, for brilliant indeed will be our career, can we but effect our object.

Our prospectus has already been acquainted with our purpose; we will here advert to it again. We propose to divide our matter into four distinct parts:—
1st.—Religious and moral instruction. 2ndly.—Local intelligence, Historical information, and facts, exclusively Jewish. 3rdly.—Original articles. 4thly—Text books.

1st. The advantages to be derived from our first division, "religious and moral instruction" must at once present themselves; for what can confer greater benefit on man, than the knowledge of his duty towards God and his fellow-creatures—what can tend so much to his spiritual welfare as the former? what contribute so much to improve his social condition as the latter? How can his happiness be better computed, than by pointing out to him, that in gratitude for the numberless benefits he receives at the hands of a gracious and merciful Providence, he is required to love his neighbour as himself, and to seek the presence of his Maker through the tenets of our holy religion;—a religion, the basis of all others, standing out in all its original purity, after the lapse of ages; while other creeds, since framed, but of man's devising, have crumbled into nought, and left no trace to tell that they have been. Time has breathed his withering blast o'er their nothingness, and like the clay that made them, they have vanished for ever.

2ndly. By local intelligence, we mean the proceedings of our many congregations at home and abroad; their exertions in the cause of religion and charity, and their progress in knowledge. What can better stimulate them to renewed efforts, than the thought, that what they have done is appreciated? and what promote the desire of doing good among us, so much as their example? Facts exclusively Jewish, will consist of anecdotes of eminent men, reports of public meetings, extracts from foreign and domestic journals, and a calendar of current festivals, fasts, &c. Our historical information will be derived from authentic records.

3rdly. For original articles, we trust partially, to the kindness of contributors; but we are assured, that we are correct in our anticipations of numerous correspondences; for we know (ourselves) of many—and there must be others, with whom we are not acquainted, who will be but too anxious to give publicity to their opinions, on subjects connected with Jewish welfare; and willing to commit

to our publication, the less matter of fact, but not less honorable productions of their well stored minds; indeed, we have already received a tale, which we purpose commencing at the earliest opportunity.

4thly. Our Text Books will not, we dare venture to assert, form the least attractive part of our information ;—nay, they will perhaps, be the most essentially useful. The הגדה; Passover service, though it does not possess the charm of novelty, will at least be acceptable, as it will contain the forms of German, Spanish, and Portuguese Jews, with the Hebrew from the Hidenheim editions, and will be carefully translated. To our Dictionary, the first English one that has appeared, we invite more particular attention. It is derived from a source, which needs but to be named, to be appreciated by every Hebrew scholar and student : the צמח דוד; a work, which for correctness, copiousness, and erudition, stands unrivalled ; but which, unfortunately, has hitherto, from its scarcity and price, been a stranger to most of our brethren ; they have thereby been deprived of a most valuable assistance in the prosecution of the study of our sacred language. This obstacle we propose to remove, by presenting the Lexicon, in a form at once useful and available to the resources of the most humble ; and to render the possession of it still more desirable, we shall give the rabinical, as well as the biblical hebrew, with translations and explanations of both.

Our creed is peace to all mankind—opposition to none, and the love of God; worshiping Him through the medium of our affections and hopes, and not our fears. We have now pointed out our intentions in the conduct of this work : we have only further to add, that it shall be our constant endeavour to render it worthy of your most liberal patronage, and to endow it with a character, at once religious, moral and instructive.

A seed is planted, and is anxiously watched by the gardener; weeds, that may obstruct its growth, are carefully plucked from around,—it is watered when rain comes not, and shielded from the too sultry heat of the summer sun ;—all is attended to that can tend to its flourishing ; and what is the result ? The gardener sees the little seed expand and spread, and eventually produce sweet flowers, wooing his gaze by their beautiful hues, and offering the grateful incense of their perfumes, to be wafted by every gale to his delighted senses ; or he beholds the luxuriant fruit tree, bowing beneath the accumulated weight of its own productions, and proffering its golden harvest, in blushes, for his acceptance. He perceives in this the return for his labours, and he adores the Providence that has blessed his work.

Readers, will you be the gardener, and make us the fruit tree?

An infant is ushered into life, and its frail form seems scarcely strong enough to contain its atom of existence; but the child is nurtured from a kindly and a genial source—the vital power dilates within him, and he becomes a man, in the image of his Divine Creator. His faculties are developed, his energies expanded, knowledge adds her giant strength, and he gives to them, his first supporters, the recompence for their toils and cares, in the accomplishment of their dearest wishes ; nay, more, he himself, learning his task from them, becomes what they were to him, the fountain of new existences. Readers, the inference is obvious—we are the child—we would become the man, a breath may raise us to maturity, a breath destroy us in our birth—but we feel you will decree us life; and further, we confidently hope, that the day is not far distant, when our little unpretending periodical will have found its way, alike, to the cheerful fire-side of the humble—the luxurious drawing room of the affluent—the closet of the student—and the approbation of the world.

Fig. 58. Front page of the first issue of the Jewish Chronicle. The paper has appeared regularly since.

Background Reading:

V. D. Lipman *Social History of the Jews in England* 1850-1950 p.45-49 (Schools); p.49-58 (Welfare); p.116-119 (Trade Unions); p.144-149 (Anglicization).

V. D. Lipman *A Century of Social Service — The History of the Board of Guardians.* (For the Jewish Association for the Protection of Girls and Women see p.247-255).

The Jewish Chronicle 1841 to 1941 — A Century of Newspaper History.

Chaim Bermant *Troubled Eden* p.84-96 (Organisations); p.123-136 (Schools):p.150-167 (The press).

24

Religious Institutions

Anglo-Jewry is often described as a remarkably homogeneous community, united in its efforts for welfare work, its support for the State of Israel, its activities on behalf of Soviet Jewry, and its maintenance of cultural institutions. However, religiously, it is divided into several different movements.

The Sephardim

More formally entitled 'The Spanish and Portuguese Jews' Congregation', the Sephardim trace their origins to the Iberian Peninsula, where Jews were expelled from Spain (1492) and Portugal (1497). Many went to Holland or to North Africa and the Middle East. It was the Dutch Sephardim who were the first to resettle in England after 1656. The community was tightly controlled by Ascamot (Regulations), issued by the Mahamad, the governing body.

24.1   1703 No Other Synagogue

No. 1. Considering how important is our Union without cauzing scandal to the people of this City, as we have been recommended by his Majesty King Charles the Second of Blessed Memory[1], it is agreed by all the Members of this Synagogue unanimously and conformably not to consent within this city of London and Suburbs (which is 4 miles distant) more than that our Synagogue called 'Saar asamaim'[2], and if thereby any person or persons of what quality soever, that shall intent to divide this Union, by separating themselves to say Prayers with ten in any place without the Synagogue, although it be not with the title of making a new one, incurrs immediately In Herem (which is pain of Excommunication) except it be in the house of bridegrooms or mourners, and the

Church Wardens shall be obliged with the help of all the commonalty to oppose such disturbers by all ways and with all force possible, and if it so be that in any time it shall be thought precise to divide it shall not be done without preceeding a general meeting of all the commonalty, and it shall not be allowed but by the two thirds of the voices, provided that it shall be always under the government of this, of 'Saar asamaim', which with the help of God, shall only serve for the Portuguese and Spanish Jews, that at present are in this City and newly may come to it and the Jews of other nations that may come, shall be admitted to say prayers if the Church Wardens shall seem meet.

The Ascamot

1. Following a plea for royal protection in 1664 against those attempting to reverse the Re-admission, the Jews were promised "the same favour as formerly they have had, so long as they demean themselves peaceably and quietly with due obedience to his Majesty's Laws, and without scandal to his Government."
2. "The Gate of Heaven", the Hebrew name of the congregation, first sited in Creechurch Lane and then in Bevis Marks.
(See Fig. 27 for an illustration of the Bevis Marks Synagogue).

Fig. 59. Seal of the Congregation   *Fig. 60. Tablets of the Law, Bevis Marks*

Initially regarded as the leaders and aristocrats of Anglo-Jewry, the Sephardim were later out-numbered by the vast influx of Ashkenazi Jews, those from Central and Eastern Europe. In 1984 there were 10 Sephardi communities in London, three in Manchester and one in Ramsgate.

156

The United Synagogue

The first Ashkenazi community was established in 1690. Following years of problems — with pauper funerals, members moving to new areas, and an increasing flow of immigrants needing financial support — the then five Ashkenazi Synagogues in London (the Great, Hambro, New, Bayswater and Central) decided to unite together. As trust funds and charitable foundations were involved, it was necessary to have the permission of the Charity Commissioners and to be ratified by Act of Parliament:

24.2 1870 Synagogues Unite

Whereas the Charity Commissioners for England and Wales, in their report to Her Majesty of their proceedings during the year one thousand eight hundred and sixty-nine, have reported that they have provisionally approved and certified (among other schemes for the application and management of charities) a scheme for the Jewish United Synagogues, and such scheme is set out in the appendix to their said report:

And whereas it is expedient that the said scheme, as the same is set out in the schedule to this Act, should be confirmed:

Be it enacted by the Queen's most Excellent Majesty, by and with the advice and consent of the Lords Spiritual and Temporal, and Commons, in this present Parliament assembled, and by the authority of the same, as follows:

1. The said scheme shall be confirmed and take effect.

"The objects of the Institution to be called the United Synagogue shall be the maintaining, erecting, founding and carrying on in London and its neighbourhood, places of worship for persons of the Jewish religion, who conform to the Polish or German ritual, the providing of means of burial of persons of the Jewish religion, the relief of poor persons of the Jewish religion, the contribution with other Jewish bodies to the maintenance of a Chief Rabbi and other ecclesiastical persons, and to the other communal duties devolving upon metropolitan congregations and other charitable purposes in connection with the Jewish religion".

(See Fig. 28 for an illustration of the Great Synagogue).

The Chief Rabbi of the Ashkenazi communities, Nathan Marcus Adler, played an important role in the formation of the United Synagogue. He and his successors not only became its religious leader, but also represented the whole of Anglo-Jewry in public life.

Fig. 61. The Rev. Dr. Nathan Marcus Adler, Chief Rabbi, 1845-1890.

Fig. 62. The Very Rev. Dr. Hermann Adler, C.V.O., Chief Rabbi, 1891-1911.

Fig. 63. The Very Rev. Dr. Joseph H. Hertz, C.H., Chief Rabbi, 1913-1946.

Fig. 64. The Very Rev. Dr. Sir Israel Brodie, K.B.E., Chief Rabbi, 1948-1965.

Fig. 65. Lord Immanuel Jakobovits, Chief Rabbi, appointed 1967.

In 1984, the United Synagogue had a membership of some 70 Synagogues in the London area, with many provincial Synagogues recognising the Chief Rabbi's authority.

The Reform

In 1840, the elders of Bevis Marks, citing the first Ascama[3], refused permission to start a branch Synagogue in the West End, where many of their wealthier members were living. In response to this decision, a number of families seceded, and established a new Synagogue together with some Ashkenazi families. At the same time they introduced various reforms into the service. They outlined their intentions in an open letter:

24.3   1841 A New Approach

We now proceed before opening the intended Place of Worship to lay a statement of the principles on which it is to be conducted. To secure decorum it is essential that the congregation should assemble before the commencement of prayers and remain until their conclusion. To facilitate this, more convenient hours are appointed for prayers; these being half-past nine in summer and ten in winter. To enable the attention of the public to be concentrated, the service is on no occasion to exceed two hours and a half. It has been found necessary to abridge slightly the prayers; the daily and Sabbath prayers have already been carefully revised, and considerable progress has been made with the festival prayers. To familiarise the rising generation with a knowledge of the great principles of our holy faith, religious discourses in the English language will form part of the morning service on Sabbaths and holydays. That offerings should interfere as little as possible with the devotional character of the place, and that they should not by occasioning interruptions to the reading of the law mar its effects, we have decided to discontinue calling up to the law. On the three great festivals, voluntary offerings will be made on the return of the law to the Ark, to be accompanied by personal compliments and limited to two objects: the relief of the poor and the support of the establishment. It is not intended by this body to recognise as sacred, days which are not ordained as such in Scripture; and consequently the service appointed for Holy Convocations is to be read only on the days thus designated. Gentlemen of other congregations have associated themselves with us, but we have resolved to read Hebrew after the manner of the Portuguese, believing it to be more correct: and to abolish the useless distinction now existing between those termed Portuguese and German Jews, we have given the intended Place of Worship the designation of West London Synagogue of British Jews. These views have been carried into effect not with any desire to separate, and through a sincere conviction that substantial improvements in the public worship are essential to the weal of our sacred religion, and that they will be the means of handing down to our children and to our children's children our holy faith in all its purity and integrity. Indeed, we are firmly convinced that their tendency will be to arrest and prevent secession from Judaism, an overwhelming evil which has at various times so widely spread among many of the most respectable families of our community. Most fervently do we cherish the hope that the effect of these improvements will be to inspire a deeper interest in, and a stronger feeling towards, our holy religion, and that their influence on the minds of the youth of either sex will be calculated to restrain them from traversing in their faith, or contemplating for a moment the fearful step of forsaking their religion.

Letter to the Elders of Bevis Marks

3. *See Text 22.1*

The initial response to this action was a herem — an excommunication — issued by the Chief Rabbi, and co-signed by members of the Beth Din of both the Ashkenazi and Sephardi communities in October 1841:

24.4   **1841 A Declaration**

Information having reached me, from which it appears that certain Persons calling themselves British Jews, publicly, and in their published Book of Prayer, reject the Oral Law, I deem it my duty to declare that, according to the Laws and Statutes held sacred by the whole House of Israel, any person or persons publicly declaring that he or they reject and do not believe in the authority of the Oral Law, cannot be permitted to have any communion with us Israelites in any religious rite or sacred act: I therefore earnestly entreat and exhort all God-fearing Jews, especially Parents, to caution and instruct all persons belonging to our Faith, that they be careful to attend to this Declaration, and that they be not induced to depart from our Holy Laws.

S. Hirschel, Chief Rabbi

We, the undersigned, fully concurring in the foregoing Doctrines, as set forth by the Reverend Solomon Hirschel, certify such our concurrence under our hands, this Twenty-fourth of Elul, 5601, A.M.

David Meldola

A. Haliva

I. Levy

A. Levy

A. L. Barnett

Fig. 66. The West London Synagogue of British Jews 1870

161

The herem was eventually lifted in March 1849. Another Reform Synagogue was established in Manchester in 1856. However it was only after the Second World War that the Reform grew into a national movement. In 1984 the Reform Synagogues of Great Britain comprised 35 congregations.

The Federation

The 1880s saw a massive migration of staunchly observant East European Jews, many of whom found the United Synagogue too anglicized. The hundreds of 'stiebls' and 'hevras' (small communities) established by the new immigrants were federated together in 1887.

24.5 1887 A New Federation

On Sunday last, the second meeting of representatives of Chevras and Minor Synagogues in East London was held at the Synagogue Chambers, Spital Square, to discuss plans for a federation of Chevras. Mr. Samuel Montagu, M.P., occupied the Chair, and there were about thirty delegates present.

The Chairman, in recapitulating the advantages to be gained by a Federation of the Chevras, said he hoped that arrangements for cheap funerals would be made with the United Synagogue, and so the large number of "pauper" funerals be reduced. He looked upon the Federation as a great strength to the orthodox party in London, as there would then be a compact body in East London who could readily make their views upon religious questions known. He wished the Chevras to try the Federation scheme as an experiment, and he would be pleased to bear the expense of the administration for the first year.

The following rules to guide the Federation were then unanimously carried:-

Name — The name of the Federation should be "The Federation of the Minor Synagogues".

Objects — I. To provide and render available to the members of the Federation the additional services of Jewish Ministers; (a) such Ministers to be the medium between the members of the

Federated Synagogues and the established Ecclesiastical Authorities of the Spanish and Portuguese Congregation and of the United Synagogue; (b) to visit at houses for the purpose of promoting the spiritual and physical welfare of the East London Jews; (c) to attend and preach at the Synagogues of the Federation, whenever it may be deemed necessary.

II. To endeavour to lessen the number of charity funerals by negotiating with the United Synagogue, or with others, for burials at moderate cost.

III. To obtain representation on the Board of Shechita.

IV. To obtain representation at the Board of Deputies.

V. To obtain representation at the Board of Guardians.

Constitution — The Board of the Federation shall consist of the following: The President and one elected member of each of the Federated Synagogues, and in addition also one elected representative for every whole number of 50 contributing adult male members in each of such synagogues.

Withdrawal from Federation — Any of the Federated Synagogues desiring to withdraw from the Federation shall only do so with the consent of two-thirds of the members of each of such synagogues at a meeting specially called for the purpose. If at such meeting the necessary majority of votes for the withdrawal be obtained, such withdrawal shall take place after six months' notice, such notice to expire at the next General Election.

Mr. J. Davidsohn asked whether it was contemplated to propose any distinguished leader of the community as President, as unless this was done, or the Chairman himself consented to become acting President, the Federation would fail for want of efficient organisation.

The Chairman in reply stated that he intended to try and induce the noble lord at the head of the affairs of the United Synagogue, or his brother, Mr. Leopold de Rothschild, to become President, and if elected he would be pleased to act as Vice-President. He had become a member of the Spital Square Synagogue in order to qualify himself for election.

It having been decided that the first meeting of the elected Board should be held at the Jewish Working Men's Club, on Sunday, December 4th, the meeting terminated with a vote of thanks to the Chair.

The Jewish Chronicle

When giving evidence before the Royal Commission on Alien Immigration, Montagu gave his reasons for founding the new movement:

24.6 1903 Montagu's Motives

I found there were different isolated minor synagogues in the East End of London which were disposed rather to quarrel among themselves and I formed the idea of amalgamating them together — quite a voluntary association — for their general benefit. The chief object was to get rid of the insanitary places of worship and to amalgamate two or three small ones together and have a suitable building. We have succeeded very well in that respect. At the present time we have 39 synagogues in the Federation, and the number of male seat-holders is 4,391, representing about 24,000 souls. They are located chiefly in Whitechapel and Stepney, Mile End and St. George's, but we also have one in Notting Hill. We cater, if I may call it, for the working classes among Jews.

The Royal Commission

In 1984, the Federation had a membership of some 33 communities in London.

Fig. 67. Sir Samuel Montagu, Baron Swaythling

The Liberals

Despite the modest reforms at the West London Synagogue, some felt the need for more experimentation, and the Jewish Religious Union was founded for this purpose. Initially it included Orthodox ministers, such as Rev. Singer, who participated in the opening service.

24.7   1902 The Inaugural Service

The Jewish Religious Union held its opening service on Saturday afternoon last at the Great Central Hotel. When the Rev. S. Singer, who conducted the service, ascended the pulpit to give out a few preliminary instructions a mixed congregation of some three or four hundred ladies and gentlemen must have faced him. A stranger entering the stately apartment where the service was held might have been excused if he failed to recognise that he was in the midst of a Jewish congregation, for the characteristic of the gathering was its divorce from almost all that we have become accustomed to associate with the Synagogue. The Synagogal trappings were, of course, absent. The Hebrew tongue had receded into a place of minor importance. Chazanuth with all of mediaeval and latter-day Judaism that is inter-twined with it, was banished from the scene. Even the Sepher Torah was conspicuous by its absence. A service without an Ark, without a cantor, almost without Hebrew! It was hard to believe that, as Mr. Montefiore claimed, it was still a Jewish service. The solemnity of the gathering was unmistakeable, and its prim dignity not a moment in doubt. The free and easy manners of the "Shool" which have come down from the time when the Synagogue was something more to the Jew than a praying-house, and which lead so easily to disorder, had given way to a stiff decorum which borders so nearly on frigidity. The Religious Union's method of approaching the Deity is different to that of the orthodox Jew. It is not the loud-voiced, emotional half-disciplined style, which roars out its petition to Providence, but the whispered dignified prayer of a restrained cathedral congregation with its regular and machine-like movements.

Sometimes, as the notes of the harmonium swept through the hall, one might have fancied oneself in a church. Anon came the impassioned periods of Mr. Montefiore, and the hearer felt himself wafted into a lecture hall, an impression which the demeanour of the people, who were strange to the form of service and sometimes seemed like on-lookers rather than part worshippers, greatly strengthened. Mr. Montefiore claims that there can be more than one sort of Jewish service. If so, why not the service of the Great Central Hotel as well as that of the New West End Synagogue? It is only a difference of type; not a difference in essence. Different minds, different kinds of prayers. Why is one set of prayers less Jewish than the other? And is it wise to insist on an unwholesome uniformity; to stereotype the prayer-book, so to speak, and to say "perish spiritually all those who prefer a different method of expressing their Judaism; let them drift anywhere — to agnosticism, to Christianity, to paganism, rather than allow a change in their service?" This was the attitude taken up by Mr. Montefiore in his sermon; and so far as it went, it was, at all events, arguable.

The congregation, who kept their hats on throughout the service, were handed a slip of paper as they entered, giving the order of service, as well as a little volume, which constitutes the Prayer Book of the Union. The service commenced with a "voluntary," after which Mr. Singer ascended the pulpit, gave a few necessary directions as to when the worshippers were expected to rise (they were to stand to the singing of a hymn by an unnamed author, but to sit to one of the Psalms), and then offered up a simple prayer, in which he claimed that the congregation had met, not in a spirit of rebellion, but in love of the faith. They were seeking the welfare of Israel, he said, and he prayed that in what they did there should be not noise and clamour, but prayer and work. No less striking than the eloquence of the prayer was the deep sincerity from which it obviously sprang. There followed the well-known verses, "In every place where I cause My name to be remembered I will come unto thee and I will bless thee," verses intended, no doubt, to form a Biblical justification for the service.

The Jewish Chronicle

Fig. 68. The inaugural service of the Jewish Religious Union 1902.

The Union soon developed a radical character and became a separate movement — Liberal Judaism — led by Claude Montefiore and Lily Montagu.

In 1984, the Union of Liberal and Progressive Synagogues comprised some 25 Synagogues throughout Great Britain.

Background Reading:

Albert M. Hyamson *The Sephardim of England.*
Aubrey Newman *The United Synagogue 1870-1970.*
Michael Leigh *Reform Judaism in England* in *Reform Judaism* (ed. D. Marmur p.3-50).
Bernard Homa *Orthodoxy in Anglo-Jewry* p.10-18.
Vivian G. Simmons *The Path of Life* p.23-33 (Liberal Judaism).
Chaim Bermant *Troubled Eden* p.178-219, 228-238.

Zionism

Zionism — a political movement working towards the re-establishment of a Jewish homeland — was founded by Theodor Herzl in 1897 at a conference in Basle. Herzl came to London to give evidence before the Royal Commission on Alien Immigration, which had been set up to review the influx of Jews from Russia:

25.1   1902 A Home for the Jews

The main principle of Zionism is that the solution of the Jewish difficulty is the recognition of Jews as a people, and the finding by them of a legally recognised home, to which Jews in those parts of the world in which they are oppressed would naturally migrate, for they would arrive there as citizens just because they are Jews, and not as aliens.

This would mean the diverting of the stream of emigration from this country and from America, where so soon as they form a perceptible number they become a trouble and a burden to a land where the true interest would be served by accommodating as many as possible.

Given to Jews their rightful position as a people, I am convinced they would develop a distinct Jewish cult — national characteristics and national aspirations — which would make for the progress of mankind.

Theodor Herzl

Following the arrival of Chaim Weizmann in Manchester in 1904, to work as a scientist there, the centre of the Zionist movement gradually shifted to England. When General Allenby's forces ended 400 years of Ottoman rule in Palestine in 1917 and Britain took charge of the country, Britain became the central arena for Zionist activity.

Fig. 69. General Allenby's triumphant entry through the Jaffa Gate of the Old City of Jerusalem 1917.

The Foreign Secretary, Arthur Balfour, wrote to Lord Rothschild:

25.2   1917 The Balfour Declaration

Dear Lord Rothschild,

I have much pleasure in conveying to you, on behalf of His Majesty's Government, the following declaration of sympathy with Jewish Zionist aspirations which has been submitted to, and approved by, the Cabinet.

"His Majesty's Government view with favour the establishment in Palestine of a national home for the Jewish people, and will use their best endeavours to facilitate the achievement of this object, it being clearly understood that nothing shall be done which may prejudice the civil and religious rights of existing non-Jewish communities in

Palestine, or the rights and political status enjoyed by Jews in any other country''.

I should be grateful if you would bring this declaration to the knowledge of the Zionist Federation.

Not all English Jews favoured Zionism, as was indicated by a letter to 'The Times':

25.3 1917 Jewish Anti-Zionists

In view of the statement and discussions lately published in the newspapers relative to a projected Jewish resettlement in Palestine on a national basis, the Conjoint Foreign Committee of the Board of Deputies of British Jews and the Anglo-Jewish Association deem it necessary to place on record the views they hold on this important question...

The claim that the Jewish settlements in Palestine shall be recognised as possessing a national character in a political sense is part and parcel of a wider Zionist theory, which regards all the Jewish communities of the world as constituting one homeless nationality, incapable of complete social and political identification, with the nations among whom they dwelt, and it is argued that for this homeless nationality, a political centre and an always available homeland in Palestine are necessary. Against this theory the Conjoint Committee strongly and earnestly protest.

Emancipated Jews in this country regard themselves primarily as a religious community, and they have always based their claims to political equality with their fellow-citizens of other creeds on this assumption and on its corollary — that they have no separate national aspirations in a political sense. They hold Judaism to be a religious system, with which their political status has no concern, and they maintain that, as citizens of the countries in which they live, they are fully and sincerely identified with the national spirit and interests of those countries. It follows that the establishment of a Jewish nationality in Palestine, founded on this theory of Jewish homelessness, must have the effect throughout the world of stamping the Jews as strangers in their native lands, and of undermining their hard-won position as citizens and nationals of those lands.

David Alexander President, *The Board of Deputies[1]*
Claude Montefiore President, *The Anglo-Jewish Association[2]*

1. *Following the furore caused by the letter within the Jewish community and a letter of repudiation by Chief Rabbi Hertz, Alexander was obliged to resign his post.*
2. *Founded in 1871, it was devoted to educational and charitable activities, and espoused the virtues of patriotism.*

In 1920, Britain was given a formal mandate to administer Palestine by the League of Nations. Sir Herbert Samuel, himself a Jew and sympathetic to the idea of a Jewish homeland, was appointed the first High Commissioner. (see front cover for an illustration of Sir Herbert Samuel).

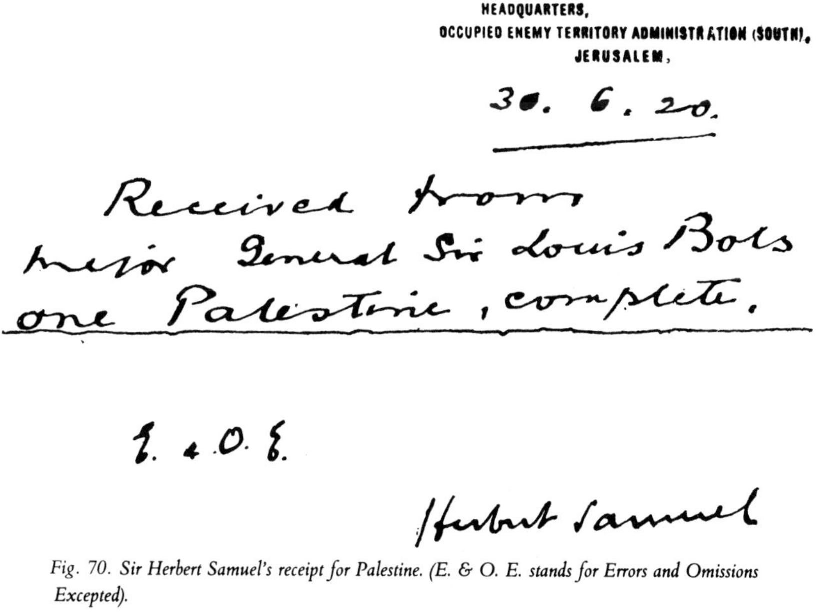

HEADQUARTERS,
OCCUPIED ENEMY TERRITORY ADMINISTRATION (SOUTH),
JERUSALEM,

30. 6. 20.

Received from Major General Sir Louis Bols one Palestine, complete.

E. & O. E.

Herbert Samuel

Fig. 70. Sir Herbert Samuel's receipt for Palestine. (E. & O. E. stands for Errors and Omissions Excepted).

Caught between Jewish and Arab nationalism, Britain found the administration of the Mandate an increasingly difficult task. The Colonial Secretary, Malcolm MacDonald, issued a White Paper on the matter:

10. In the light of these considerations His Majesty's Government make the following declaration of their intentions regarding the future government of Palestine: (1) The objective of His Majesty's Government is the establishment within ten years of an independent Palestine State in such treaty relations with the United Kingdom as will provide satisfactorily for the commercial and strategic requirements of both countries in the future. This proposal for the establishment of the independent State would involve consultation with the Council of the League of Nations with a view to the termination of the Mandate. (2) The independent State should be one in which Arabs and Jews share in government in such a way as to ensure that the essential interests of each community are safeguarded

...

II. (Immigration)

12. If immigration has an adverse effect on the economic position in the country, it should clearly be restricted; and equally, if it has a seriously damaging effect on the political position in the country, that is a factor that should not be ignored. Although it is not difficult to contend that the large number of Jewish immigrants who have been admitted so far have been absorbed economically, the fear of the Arabs that this influx will continue indefinitely until the Jewish population is in a position to dominate them has produced consequences which are extremely grave for Jews and Arabs alike and for the peace and prosperity of Palestine. The lamentable disturbances of the past three years are only the latest and most sustained manifestation of this intense Arab apprehension. The methods employed by Arab terrorists against fellow-Arabs and Jews alike must receive unqualified condemnation. But it cannot be denied that fear of indefinite Jewish immigration is widespread amongst the Arab population and that this fear has made possible disturbances which have given a serious setback to economic progress, depleted the Palestine exchequer, rendered life and property insecure, and produced a bitterness between the Arab and Jewish populations which is deplorable between citizens of the same country.

14. It has been urged that all further Jewish immigration into Palestine should be stopped forthwith. His Majesty's Government cannot accept such a proposal. It would damage the whole of the financial and economic system of Palestine and thus affect adversely the interests of Arabs and Jews alike. Moreover, in the view of His Majesty's Government, abruptly to stop further immigration would be unjust to the Jewish National Home. But, above all, His Majesty's Government are conscious of the present unhappy plight of large numbers of Jews who seek a refuge from certain European countries, and they believe that Palestine can and should make a further contribution to the solution of this pressing world problem. In all these circumstances, they believe that they will be acting consistently with their Mandatory obligations to both Arabs and Jews, and in the manner best calculated to serve the interests of the whole people of Palestine, by adopting the following proposals regarding immigration: (1) Jewish immigration during the next five years will be at a rate which, if economic absorptive capacity permits, will bring the Jewish population up to approximately one-third of the total population of the country. Taking into account the expected natural increase of the Arab and Jewish populations, and the number of illegal Jewish immigrants now in the country, this would allow of the admission, as from the beginning of April this year, of some 75,000 immigrants over the next five years ...

15. His Majesty's Governnment are satisfied that, when the immigration over five years which is now contemplated has taken place, they will not be justified in facilitating, nor will they be under any obligation to facilitate, the further development of the Jewish National Home by immigration regardless of the wishes of the Arab population.

The White Paper was seen as a repudiation of the Balfour Declaration and as appeasement of the Arabs, and was condemned by the Jewish Agency[3]:

25.5   1939 White Paper Rejected

1. The effect of the new policy for Palestine laid down by the

Mandatory Government in the White Paper of May 17, 1939, is to deny to the Jewish people the right to reconstitute their National Home in their ancestral country. It is a policy which transfers authority over Palestine to the present Arab majority, puts the Jewish population at the mercy of that majority, decrees the stoppage of Jewish immigration as soon as the Jewish inhabitants form one-third of the total (population), and sets up a territorial ghetto for the Jews in their own homeland.

5. It is in the darkest hours of Jewish history that the British Government proposes to deprive the Jews of their last hope, and to close the road back to their homeland. It is a cruel blow; doubly cruel because it comes from the Government of a great nation which has extended a helping hand to Jews, and whose position in the world rests upon foundations of moral authority and international good faith. This blow will not subdue the Jewish people. The historic bond between the people and the land of Israel will not be broken. The Jews will never accept the closing against them of the gates of Palestine, nor let their national home be converted into a ghetto. Jewish pioneers, who in the past three generations have shown their strength in the upbuilding of a derelict country, will from now on display the

Fig. 71. Plaque at 67 Addison Road, London W.14, where Weizmann resided for some years.

same strength in defending Jewish immigration, the Jewish home, and Jewish freedom.

3.   The official body set up by the League of Nations to advise on the establishment of a Jewish national homeland.

The war years prevented any decision being made, although lobbying for and against a Jewish state continued. Following the United Nations vote in November 1947 to bring a Jewish homeland into existence, Britain withdrew from Palestine and the State of Israel was declared on 14th May 1948.

Background Reading:
Martin Gilbert *Exile and Return — The Emergence of Jewish Statehood.*

Fig. 72. General Allenby, Lord Balfour and Sir Herbert Samuel at the opening of the Hebrew University, Jerusalem, 1st April 1925. Courtesy of Martin Gilbert.

26

Recent Decades

The 1930s saw the rise of Fascism in Germany and Italy, and Sir Oswald Mosley tried to import it to England through his British Union of Fascists. The Fascist meetings were always characterised by violence and anti-semitism. When Mosley announced that the Fascists would march through Jewish areas of the East End, the local residents, Jews and non-Jews, rejected the Board of Deputies' advice to ignore him, and determined to block his path.

26.1 1936 The Battle of Cable Street

I was at Gardiner's Corner when, on that bright autumn morning 3,000 Blackshirts mobilised on their start line in Royal Mint Street poised to march out in four columns by way of Cable Street. Their flanks were to be protected en route by nearly 7,000 policemen recruited into the area and including the entire Metropolitan corps of mounted police. Radio vans patrolled and an autogyro flew overhead to monitor the opposing forces. At the confluence of Cable and Leman Street barricades were being erected and a huge crowd collected at Gardiners Corner — the real point of entry into East London. By mid-afternoon it was estimated that a hostile army of at least 100,000 had gathered along the proposed route. Anti-fascist placards hung from windows and walls; and the current slogan of the Spanish Republic 'THEY SHALL NOT PASS!' was proclaimed everywhere on a sea of banners. The 'battle of Cable Street' broke out when a lorry dragged from a yard was overturned in the middle of the road, forming the base of a barricade. Police charges were met by a hail of stones and bricks from defenders on the ground and from the upper storeys of surrounding houses. It was the dockers of Wapping and St. George's who constituted the vanguard of opposition here, thus preventing the march from taking off. After some police skirmishing and subsequent injuries and arrests, Sir Phillip Game, Commissioner of Police, was convinced that it would be impossible for Mosley to proceed without mass riots and bloodshed. He ordered Mosley to turn about and the procession marched off to the music of pipes and drums, in the opposite direction, along the Embankment, where, in the absence of an audience, they quickly dispersed. That night there was dancing in the side streets as East Enders celebrated their victory and the birth of a 'heroic' legend.

William J. Fishman *The Streets of East London*

An immediate result of the 'battle' was the Public Order Act, which prohibited political uniforms and gave the police powers to ban processions. This Act, and the growing troubles in Europe, led to the decline of the British Union. In the 1960s and 1970s, other right-wing groups, particularly the National Front, attempted to gain public support, but were unsuccessful both at the polls and in the streets.

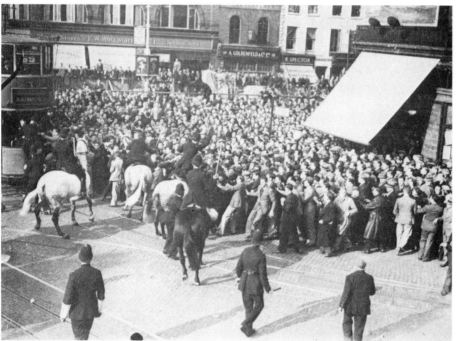

Fig. 73. Mounted police attempt to clear the road at Gardiner's Corner 1936.

When Britain declared war on Germany in 1939, some 75,000 refugees had already arrived in the country, the vast majority of whom had fled from Nazi oppression. Despite the opposition of the refugees to all that Germany had stood for, to British eyes they were indistinguishable from all other Germans. Calls for the internment of the "aliens" came not only from the general public, but also from the Chiefs of Staff:

26.2   1940 Internment Advised

... the most ruthless action should be taken to eliminate any chance of fifth column activities, including the internment of all enemy aliens and of all members of subversive organisations. Alien refugees are a most dangerous source of subversive activity. The number of new refugees admitted to Britain must be cut to the minimum and those admitted must be kept under closest surveillance.

... to leave such a considerable proportion of enemy aliens at large at a time like this seems to us to be taking unwarranted risks. From a purely military point of view we consider that *all* should be detained forthwith on the understanding that those who can be proved beyond all doubt to be harmless could be released subsequently.

Memorandum to the War Cabinet

Fig. 74. "Friendly Aliens Avenue" at Onchan Camp, Isle of Man 1941

Some 5,000 Jews were deported to Canada and Australia, while another 15,000 were interned on the Isle of Man or elsewhere in Britain. An outcry against this injustice led to the end of internment after a few months, and the majority went into war work, the Pioneer Corps or other units.

Religious controversies have been rare in Anglo-Jewry. The 'Jacobs Affair' was the first to have an impact on the community since the secession of the Reform. A strictly orthodox Jew and a member of the United Synagogue Rabbinate, Jacobs tried to harmonise traditional Judaism with a modern approach to the Bible.

26.3   1962 The Jacobs Affair

The view I have tried to sketch briefly in this book and have tried to elaborate on in subsequent books, that the Jew, if he is not to stifle his reason, must be free to investigate the classical sources of Judaism with as much objectivity as he can command and should not look upon this as precluded by his religious faith, seems to me to be impregnable. Needless to say, this is not my discovery but is held by the vast majority of Jewish scholars of any academic repute. The result of such investigation, involving the use of tried methods of research, a cautious weighing of the evidence and an unbiased approach to the texts, yields a picture of the Bible and the Talmud as works produced by human beings, bearing all the marks of human literary production, influenced in style, language and ideas by the cultural background of their day. Like other human productions they contain error as well as truth. For all that, and this is the most significant part of the discussion for faith, the believer can still see the Torah as divine revelation. The notion of divine dictation must, of course, be abandoned, once the human element is granted, and the Bible, for example, can no longer be seen as revelation itself. But it is the record of revelation. The whole is a tremendous account (and for this reason unique and not simply 'inspired' in the sense in which one speaks of Shakespeare or Beethoven being inspired) of the divine-human encounter in the history of our ancestors in which they reached out gropingly for God and He responded to their faltering quest. This does not mean that we can naively mark (as I have been accused of trying to do) certain lofty passages as divine and others of a more primitive nature as human. In the new picture of the Bible the divine and the human are seen as intertwined. Because humans had a hand in its composition it is, from one point of view, all human. Because out of its totality God is revealed to us and speaks to us, it is, from another point of view, all divine.

Louis Jacobs *We Have Reason To Believe*

In the resulting furore, Jacobs resigned his position as Tutor at Jews' College and eventually established his own community, the New London Synagogue. The controversy received wide publicity in the British press and for a time it was thought that a new movement would be formed. Although many sympathised with Jacobs, no real support materialised until the 1980s when the Conservative (Masorti) movement was formed around his teaching.

Fig. 75. Rabbi Dr. Louis Jacobs addressing the meeting of members of the New West End Synagogue at which a resolution was passed to form the New London Synagogue, 1964.

While many English Jews had given much support to Israel ever since the State had been established, the Six Day War had an electrifying effect on Anglo-Jewry. The conflict awakened the community to the dangers that the State faced and the opportunities it presented. A wave of enthusiasm swept over almost everyone, even those previously indifferent or hostile to Israel. Massive fund-raising, blood collections and a rush of volunteers was the immediate response. Although this intensity waned afterwards, the reverberations of the Six Day War were profound: Israel entered into the forefront of Anglo-Jewish life and gave a raison d'être to many otherwise uncommitted Jews.

Fig. 76. The St. Johns Wood Synagogue transformed into a hospital to collect blood for Israel.

26.4   1967 The Six Day War

A RIGHT TO LIVE

Sir, — Israel is a country the size of Wales. Today it is mobilised to prevent itself becoming another Auschwitz. The Arab states which surround it have declared their intention of exterminating it. There are two-and-a-half million people in

Israel whose right to live is threatened. Behind the political game, this is what the present crisis is about. This is the basic human fact.

Signed by 36 Anglo-Jewish writers, poets and dramatists — Danni Abse, A. Alvarez, Alexander Baron, Chaim Bermant, Myrna Blumberg, Caryl Brahms, Ronald Cass, Gerda Charles, Sid Colin, David Daiches, Lionel Davidson, Marty Feldman, T. R. Fyvel, Larry Gelbart, Diana & Meir Gillon, Martyn Goff, Lewis Greifer, John Gross, Ronald Harwood, Dan Jacobson, Bernard Kops, Philip Levene, Emmanuel Litvinoff, Wolf Mankowitz, Stanley Mann, Louis Marks, Robert Muller, Denis Norden, Harold Pinter, Frederick Raphael, Mordecai Richler, Jeremy Robson, Reuben Ship, Jacob Sonntag, George Steiner.

Letter to *The Sunday Times* **the day before war broke out, signed by 36 Anglo-Jewish writers, poets and dramatists.**

Public discretion and an ever-present reluctance to be conspicuous had long been the hallmark of Anglo-Jewry — a legacy from the days of the resettlement[1]. This discretion was suddenly reversed in the 1960s and 1970s when efforts were mounted to obtain the release of Russian Jews who wanted to leave the Soviet Union, but who were prevented from emigrating. Demonstrations, marches, petitions, lobbying of M.P.'s and letters to newspapers were all used to bring public pressure on the Soviet authorities.

26.5   **1967 Soviet Jewry Campaign**

The visit of the Soviet Premier, Mr. A. N. Kosygin, is welcome as a sign of closer relations between Britain and the U.S.S.R. and will, we hope, make a substantial contribution to the peaceful solution of problems that threaten our very survival.

This encourages us to make a further appeal to the Soviet Premier on behalf of the three million Soviet Jews who have not yet been given facilities to rebuild their national existence, shattered by the war and the destruction of Soviet-Jewish institutions in 1948, on a level of equality with other nationalities. At present there are no schools or classes in which

Jewish children may study their own history, literature and traditions.

Although the Soviet Union has the largest Yiddish-speaking population in the world, Jewish cultural resources are restricted to a handful of books and a single Yiddish journal of substance. There is no permanent Jewish theatre and no newspaper to serve the needs of the Jewish population. Hundreds of synagogues have been closed, and Jewish worshippers are more stringently restricted in their religious facilities than members of other recognised religions.

We believe it is a matter of simple justice that a community which suffered destruction by war and intolerance should be given the opportunity to ensure its survival and we are hopeful that this belief will also commend itself to Mr. Kosygin.

Letter to *The Times* **from David Daiches and others.**

1. See Chapter 22, Note 1.

Since 1968, some 300,000 Jews have been able to leave Russia, going largely to Israel and the United States. With thousands more still refused an exit visa, and often subject to arrest and harassment, the Soviet Jewry campaign still continues for their release.

Fig. 77. Demonstration on behalf of Soviet Jews outside the office of the communist daily newspaper Morning Star, 1972.

Today the estimated population of Anglo-Jewry is 353,000, of whom over half live in Greater London, and the remainder are scattered in some 80 provincial communities. Well represented in all aspects of public life, the business world, industry, science, academic life, the arts, entertainments, law and medicine, Anglo-Jewry is thoroughly integrated in the life of the country while still retaining its distinctive identity[2].

2. For a comprehensive list of prominent members of Anglo-Jewry, see "Who's Who" in the "Jewish Year Book".

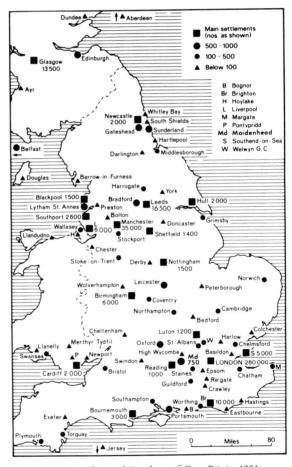

Fig. 78. The Jewish Population of Great Britain, 1984

Further Reading:

Chaim Bermant *Point of Arrival* p.231-236 (Battle of Cable Street).

Martin Walker *The National Front.*

Ronald Stent *A Bespattered Page ? — The Internment of His Majesty's Most Loyal Enemy Aliens.*

Chaim Bermant *Troubled Eden* p.239-253 (The Jacobs Affair); p.111-122 (Zionism).

Elie Wiesel *The Jews of Silence* (Soviet Jewry) and see publications of National Council for Soviet Jewry.

Sources

(See Bibliography for full reference details)

Abbreviation : *J.A.E.* = *Jews of Angevin England*

1.1 Anthony à Wood i., p.129 Fuller, Camb., p.8; quoted J. Jacobs *J.A.E.* p.4

1.2 *Domesday* 154, 160b; quoted J. Jacobs *J.A.E.* p.5

1.3 William of Malmesbury *Gesta Rerum Anglicanarum* iv 317 ed. Duffy p.500; quoted J. Jacobs *J.A.E.* p.6

2.1 St. Anselm *Opera* ed. 1744 tom.ii.p.255; quoted J. Jacobs *J.A.E.* p.7

2.2 Jocelin de Brakeland *Chronica* ed. Rokewood (Cam. Soc.) p.8; quoted J. Jacobs *J.A.E.* p.78

2.3 Elhanan ben Isaac *Tosaphot* Halberstamm MS. f.48b; quoted J. Jacobs *J.A.E.* p.269

2.4 J. C. Robertson *Materials for History of Thomas Beckett* ii.7; quoted J. Jacobs *J.A.E.* p.153

2.5 Mordecai ben Hillel *Sefer Mordecai* ii.826; quoted J. Jacobs *J.A.E.* p.54

2.6 Judah ben Eliezer *Minhat Yehuda* Halberstamm MS. No. 345 f.40a; quoted J. Jacobs *J.A.E.* p.288

2.7 Roger de Hovedene *Chronica* ii.,137; quoted J. Jacobs *J.A.E.* p.62

2.8 Roger de Hovedene *Chronica* ii.,261; quoted J. Jacobs *J.A.E.* p.75

2.9 *Charter Rolls* i.7; quoted J. Jacobs *J.A.E.* p.202

2.10 Norwich Betrothal Contract; quoted M. D. Davis *Hebrew Deeds of English Jews* p.33 translated by J. A. Romain

2.11 Gudemann *Geschichte* i.267; quoted J. Jacobs *J.A.E.* p.243

3.1 *Charter Rolls* i.93; quoted J. Jacobs *J.A.E.* p.212

4.1	*Old English Chronicles* Peterborough MS.; quoted J. Jacobs *J.A.E.* p.19
4.2	Geoffrey Chaucer *The Canterbury Tales,* translated by Nevill Coghill (Penguin Books, London 1951)
4.3	Plaque at Lincoln Cathedral
5.1	Giraldus Cambrensis *Vita S. Remigii Opera* vii. p.36; quoted J. Jacobs *J.A.E.* p.57
5.2	*Pipe Rolls* 9 Richard I; quoted J. Jacobs *J.A.E.* p.58
5.3	Record Office, Misc. Q.R. 556.1; quoted J. Jacobs *J.A.E.* p.66
5.4	Walsingham *Gesta Abbatium St. Albani* ed. Riley 193; quoted J. Jacobs *J.A.E.* p.79
5.5	Benedict the Abbot *Gesta Henrici* ed. Stubbs ii.p.5; quoted J. Jacobs *J.A.E.* p.91
6.1	William of Newbury *Historia Rerum Anglicanarum* ed.Howlett i.p.294; quoted J. Jacobs *J.A.E.* p.99
7.1	William of Newbury *Historia Rerum Anglicanarum* ed. Howlett i.p.312; quoted J. Jacobs *J.A.E.* p.117
8.1	*Magna Carta*
9.1	*Mandate to the Justices* 31st January 1253; quoted J. M. Rigg *Select Pleas, Starrs* p.xlviii
10.1	*Statutum de Judeismo*; see Statutes of the Realm i.220
11.1	*Writ to the Sheriff of Gloucester* 18th July 1290; see *Foedera* ed. Rymer
11.2	*Salvus conductus pro omnibus Judeis* 27th July 1290; quoted *Foedera* ed. Rymer (1816) vol.1,p.736 translated J. A. Romain
12.1	Protocol for 27th December 1540 quoted L. Wolf *Essays in Jewish History* p.81
12.2	Processo 9449 Inquisition of Lisbon quoted C. Roth *The Case of Thomas Fernandes* in *Miscellanies* II p.32ff
13.1	Christopher Marlowe *The Jew of Malta* Act II Scene III line 20ff
13.2	Christopher Marlowe *The Jew of Malta* Act II Scene III line 178ff
13.3	Christopher Marlowe *The Jew of Malta* Act II Scene III line 313
13.4	Christopher Marlowe *The Jew of Malta* Act IV Scene IV line 76
13.5	William Shakespeare *The Merchant of Venice* Act I Scene III line 30ff
13.6	William Shakespeare *The Merchant of Venice* Act III Scene I line 55ff

1833; quoted *Macaulay on Jewish Disabilities* (ed.I. Abrahams & S. Levy) pp.47,52.56

18.2 *Act for the Relief of Persons of the Jewish Religion elected to Municipal Offices* (31st July 1845) 8 & 9 Vict. c.52

18.3 Quoted C. Bermant *The Cousinhood* p.95

18.4 *An Act to provide for the Relief of Her Majesty's Subjects professing the Jewish Religion* (23rd July 1858)21 & 22 Vict.c.49

18.5 *The Jewish Chronicle* 8th February 1861 p.4; quoted G. Alderman *The Jewish Community in British Politics* p.30

18.6 *Punch* 12th December 1868

19.1 Moses Cassuto *The Travels of Moses Cassuto*; quoted J. M. Shaftesley (ed.) *Remember The Days* p.103

19.2 Minutes of the Board of Deputies 1802; quoted C. H. L. Emmanuel *A Century and a Half of Jewish History* p.10

19.3 Letter of Joshua van Oven to Patrick Colquhoun 24th March 1801; quoted C. Roth *Anglo-Jewish Letters* p.213

19.4 Samuel Taylor Coleridge; quoted R. D. Barnett "Anglo-Jewry in the Eighteenth Century" in V. D. Lipman *Three Centuries of Anglo-Jewry* p.62

19.5 E. P. Marks *The Key to the Sacred Language, being a concise though comprehensive Orthographical and Orthoepical Hebrew and English Grammar, with points* (London 1818); quoted C. Roth *Essays and Portraits in Anglo-Jewry* p.228

19.6 Quoted C. Roth ibid p.214

19.7 *The Christian Turned Jew, Being the most Remarkable Life and Adventures of Lord George Gordon*; quoted C. Roth ibid p.190

20.1 Sir Walter Scott *Ivanhoe* (1819) Chapter XXXIII

20.2 Sir Walter Scott *Ivanhoe* (1819) Chapter XXVIII

20.3 Lord Byron *Hebrew Melodies* (1815)

20.4 Charles Dickens *Oliver Twist* (1837) Chapter IX

20.5 Charles Dickens *Our Mutual Friend* (1863) Book II Chapter V

20.6 Charles Dickens *Our Mutual Friend* (1863) Book IV Chapter IX

20.7 George Eliot *Daniel Deronda* (1876) Chapter XLII

21.1 Beatrix Potter in *The Life and Labour of the People* by Charles Booth Vol I 1889 p.581–3

21.2 Myer Wilchinski *History of a Sweater*; quoted W. J. Fishman *East End Jewish Radicals* p.46

21.3 *The Lancet* 11th June 1888

21.4 quoted J. White *Rothschild Buildings* p.35

21.5   quoted J. White *Rothschild Buildings* p.42

21.6   quoted J. White *Rothschild Buildings* p.59

21.7   quoted J. White *Rothschild Buildings* p.97

21.8   Medical Officer of Health of London County Council *Report of the Royal Commission on Alien Immigration* 1902-3

21.9   Beatrix Potter in *The Life and Labour of the People* by Charles Booth Vol I 1889 p.204

21.10   quoted J. White *Rothschild Buildings* p.139

21.11   *HaMeliz* XXVIII 287 (Dec.30, 1888-Jan.11, 1889); quoted L. P. Gartner *The Jewish Immigrant* p.24

21.12   Rev. G. S. Reaney in *The Destitute Alien in Great Britain* (ed. A. White, London 1892) p.87; quoted W. J. Fishman *East End Jewish Radicals* p.75

21.13   *Report of the Royal Commission on Alien Immigration* 1902-3, II Minutes of Evidence, Cd. 1742, Min. 1724

21.14   *Aliens Act* 1905; quoted V. D. Lipman *Social History of the Jews in England 1850-1950* p.141

21.15   quoted V. D. Lipman *Social History of the Jews in England 1850-1950* p.141

21.16   Beatrice Potter in *The Life and Labour of the People of London* (ed. C. Booth) p.219

22.1   *London Gazette* No. 7995 7–10th March 1740; quoted Bill Williams *The Making of Manchester Jewry*, p.3

22.2   *Sunderland Echo* 17th August 1914

22.3   Communal circular distributed in Glasgow 26th December 1913; quoted Kenneth Collins (ed.) *Aspects of Scottish Jewry* p.105

22.4   quoted Kenneth Collins (ed.) ibid. pp. 68, 82

23.1   *The Jewish Chronicle* 8th July 1898

23.2   *The Jewish Chronicle* 15th July 1898

23.3   *The Jewish Chronicle* 8th July 1898

23.4   *The Jewish Chronicle* 15th July 1898

23.5   *The Jewish Chronicle* 8th July 1898

23.6   *The Jewish Chronicle* 29th July 1898

23.7   quoted Jeffrey Gale "The Settlement Synagogue" in *North London Progressive Synagogue Newsletter,* April 1984

23.8   *Rules of the Hebrew Cabinet Makers Association* (London 1887)

24.1   Ascamot of 1703; quoted M. Gaster *History of the Ancient Synagogue of the Spanish and Portuguese Jews* p.14

24.2   *Act for confirming a Scheme of the Charity Commissioners for the Jewish United Synagogues* (14th July 1870) 33 & 34 Vict. c.116; quoted A. Newman *The United Synagogue* plate 1

24.3   *Letter to the Elders of Bevis Marks* 24th August 1841; quoted J. Picciotto *Sketches of Anglo-Jewish History* p.375

24.4   Solomon Hirschel and others 14th October 1841; quoted A. M. Hyamson *The Sephardim of England* p.287

24.5   *The Jewish Chronicle* 11th November 1887

24.6   *Report of Royal Commission on Alien Immigration* 1902-3 Q.16,772; quoted V. D. Lipman *Social History of the Jews in England* p.121

24.7   *The Jewish Chronicle* 24th October 1902

25.1   *Report of the Royal Commission on Alien Immigration* 1902-3; quoted M. Gilbert *Exile and Return* p.56

25.2   Letter of 2nd November 1917; quoted M. Gilbert *Exile and Return* p.108

25.3   *The Times* 24th May 1917; quoted *The Jew in the Modern World* (ed. Mendes-Flohr) p.456

25.4   Palestine White Paper 17th May 1939; quoted *The Jew in the Modern World* (ed. Mendes-Flohr) p.467

25.5   Jewish Agency 17th May 1939; quoted *The Jew in the Modern World* (ed. Mendes-Flohr) p.469

26.1   W. J. Fishman *The Streets of East London* p.128

26.2   Memorandum 27th May and 19th June 1940; quoted R. Stent *A Bespattered Page ?* p.70,73

26.3   L. Jacobs *We Have Reason To Believe* (1965 ed.) p.139

26.4   *The Sunday Times* 4th June 1967

26.5   *The Times* 13th February 1967; quoted *Jews in Eastern Europe* (ed. E. Litvinoff) vol. III no. 6 May 1967 p.5

Illustrations

Cover: Rabbi Manasseh ben Israel presents his petition to Oliver Cromwell. Now believed destroyed. Solomon Hart.

The title-page depicts "Zachariah and his wife" from the Holkham Bible, 14th century.

194

Bibliography

The following works are cited in the text and/or notes above

Abrahams, Israel   *Jewish Life in the Middle Ages* Atheneum, New York 1973

Abrahams I. and Levy S.   *Macaulay on Jewish Disabilities* Jewish Historical Society of England, Edinburgh 1909

Alderman, Geoffrey   *The Jewish Community in British Politics* Oxford University Press, Oxford 1983

Barnett, Richard B. and Levy, Abraham   *The Bevis Marks Synagogue* Society of Heshaim, London 1975

Bermant, Chaim   *Point of Arrival* Methuen, London 1975 *The Cousinhood* Eyre and Spottiswoode, London 1971 *Troubled Eden* Vallentine Mitchell, London 1969

Booth, Charles   *Life and Labour of the People of London* London 1902

Collins, Kenneth E.   *Aspects of Scottish Jewry* Glasgow Jewish Representative Council, Glasgow 1987

Croner, Gerald (ed.)   *England* Keter Books, Jerusalem 1978

Davis, M.D.   *Hebrew Deeds of English Jews* 1888, reprinted Gregg International Publishers, Israel 1969

Dobson, R.B.   *The Jews of Medieval York and the Massacre of March 1190* St. Anthony's Hall Publications, York 1974

Emanuel, C.H.L.   *A Century and a Half of Jewish History Extracted from the Minute Books of the London Committee of Deputies of the British Jews* London 1910

Encyclopaedia Judaica   Keter, Jerusalem 1972

Fisch, Harold   *The Dual Image — A Study of the Jew in*

	English Literature World Jewish Library, London 1971
Fishman, William J.	*East End Jewish Radicals 1875-1914* Duckworth, London 1975 *The Streets of East London* Duckworth, London 1979
Gaster, Moses	*History of the Ancient Synagogue of the Spanish and Portuguese Jews* London 1901
Gartner, Lloyd P.	*The Jewish Immigrant in England 1870-1914* Simon Publications, London 1973
Gilbert, Martin	*Exile and Return* Weidenfeld and Nicolson, London 1978 *Jewish History Atlas* Weidenfeld and Nicolson, London 1976
Goodman, Paul	*Moses Montefiore* Jewish Publication Society of America, Philadelphia 1925
Homa, Bernard	*Orthodoxy in Anglo-Jewry 1880-1940* Jewish Historical Society of Great Britain, London 1969
Hyamson, Albert M.	*The Sephardim of England* Methuen, London 1951
Jacobs, Joseph	*The Jews of Angevin England* London 1893, reprinted Gregg International Publishers, Farnborough, Hants 1969
Jacobs, Louis	*We Have Reason To Believe* Vallentine Mitchell, London 1965
The Jewish Chronicle 1841-1941	Jewish Chronicle, London 1949
Katz, David S.	*Philo-Semitism and the Readmission of the Jews to England 1603-1655* Oxford University Press, Oxford 1982
Kobler, Franz	*Letters of Jews Through the Ages* Ararat, London 1952
Levy, Arnold	*History of the Sunderland Jewish Community* Macdonald, London 1956
Lipman, V. D.	*A Century of Social Service 1859-1959 — The History of the Jewish Board of Guardians* Routledge and Kegan Paul, London 1959 *Social History of the Jews in England 1850-1950* Watts, London 1954 *Three Centuries of Anglo-Jewish History*

	Jewish Historical Society of England, London 1961
Loewe, Louis	*Diaries of Sir Moses and Lady Montefiore* Jewish Historical Society of England, London 1983
Marcus, Jacob R.	*The Jew in the Medieval World* Atheneum, New York 1974
Marmur, Dow (ed.)	*Reform Judaism* Reform Synagogues of Great Britain, London 1973
Mendes-Flohr, Paul & Reinharz, Jehudah	*The Jew in the Modern World* Oxford University Press 1980
Modder, Montagu Frank	*The Jew in the Literature of England* Jewish Publication Society of America, Philadelphia 1960
Newman, Aubrey	*The United Synagogue 1870-1970* Routledge and Kegan Paul, London 1977
Picciotto, James	*Sketches of Anglo-Jewish History* 1875, reprinted Soncino Press, London 1956
Richardson H.G.	*The English Jewry under Angevin Kings* Jewish Historical Society of England, London 1960
Rigg, J.M.	*Select Pleas, Starrs and other records from the Exchequer of the Jews 1220-1284* Jewish Historical Society of England London 1902
Roth, Cecil	*Anglo-Jewish Letters* Soncino Press, London 1938 *Essays and Portraits in Anglo-Jewish History* Jewish Publication Society of America, Philadelphia 1962 *A History of the Jews in England* Clarendon Press, Oxford 1964 *A History of the Marranos* Schocken, New York 1974 *The Case of Thomas Fernandes* in *Miscellanies II* Jewish Historical Society of England, London *The Great Synagogue, London 1690-1940* Edward Goldston, London 1950
Salbstein, M.C.N.	*The Emancipation of the Jews in Britain — The Question of the Admission of the Jews to Parliament 1828-1860* The Littman Library of Jewish Civilization, London 1982

Shaftesley, John M.	*Remember The Days* Jewish Historical Society of England, London 1966
Simmons, Vivian G.	*The Path of Life* Vallentine Mitchell, London 1961
Stent, Ronald	*A Bespattered Page — The Internment of 'His Majesty's Most Loyal Aliens'* Andre Deutsch, London 1980
The Jewish Year Book	Jewish Chronicle, London published annually
Walker, Martin	*The National Front* Fontana, London 1978
White, Jerry	*Rothschild Buildings — Life in an East End Tenement Block 1887-1920* Routledge and Kegan Paul, London 1980
Wiesel, Elie	*The Jews of Silence* Signet Books, New York 1967
Williams, Bill	*The Making of Manchester Jewry* Manchester University Press, Manchester 1976
Wolf, Lucien	*Essays in Jewish History* Jewish Historical Society of England, London 1934 *Manasseh ben Israel's mission to Oliver Cromwell. Being a reprint of the pamphlets published by Manasseh ben Israel to promote the readmission of the Jews to England 1649-1656* London 1901

Further Reading

(*) denotes those suitable for children of 10-13 years
(P) denotes play

A. NON-FICTION

Abrahams, Beth Zion	*The Jews in England* (*) Vallentine Mitchell, London 1969
Abse, Dannie	*Ash on a Young Man's Sleeve* Vallentine Mitchell, London 1969
Aris, Stephen	*The Jews in Business* Jonathan Cape, London 1970
Bild, Ian	*The Jews in Britain* Batsford Educational London 1984
Cowan, Evelyn	*Spring Remembered — A Scottish Jewish Childhood* T & A Constable, Edinburgh 1974
Daiches, David	*Two Worlds — An Edinburgh Childhood* Harcourt Brace, New York 1956
Emden, Paul	*Jews of Britain — A Series of Biographies* Sampson Low, London 1943
Endelman, Todd	*The Jews of Georgian England* Jewish Publication Society of America, Philadelphia 1979
Grunfield, Judith	*Shefford — The Story of a Jewish School Community in Evacuation 1939-1945* Soncino Press, London 1980
Homa, Bernard	*Fortress in Anglo-Jewry — The Story of the Machzike Hadath* Shapiro Vallentine, London 1953
Krausz, Ernest	*Leeds Jewry* Jewish Historical Society of England, London 1964

Levin, S. S.	*A Century of Anglo-Jewish Life 1870-1970* The United Synagogue, London 1971
Lipman, V. D.	*The Jews of Medieval Norwich* Jewish Historical Society of England, London 1967
Litvinoff, Emanuel	*Journey Through a Small Planet* Michael Joseph, London 1972
Kops, Bernard	*The World is a Wedding* Macgibbon & Kee, London 1963
Moonman, Jane	*Anglo-Jewry — An Analysis* Joint Israel Appeal, London 1980
Pollins, Harold	*Economic History of the Jews in England* Associated University Presses, London 1982
Roth, Cecil	*The Jewish Contribution to Civilisation* Macmillan, London 1938
Rubens, Alfred	*A History of Jewish Costume* Vallentine Mitchell, London 1967
Transactions	published regularly by the Jewish Historical Society of England
Williams, Bill	*The Making of Manchester Jewry* 1740-1875 Manchester University Press 1976

B. FICTION

Golding, Louis	*Magnolia Street* Arrow, London 1957
Kops, Bernard	*The Hamlet of Stepney Green* (P) Penguin, London 1968 *The Dissent of Dominic Shapiro* Macgibbon & Kee, London 1956
Mankowitz, Wolf	*A Kid for Two Farthings* (P) Andre Deutsch, London 1953
Melnikoff, Pamela	*The Star and The Sword* (*) Vallentine Mitchell, London 1965
Mosco, Maisie	*Almonds and Raisins* New English Library, London 1979 *Scattered Seed* New English Library, London 1980 *Children's Children* New English Library, London 1981 *Between Two Worlds* New English Library, London 1983

Rosenthal, Jack	*The Barmitzvah Boy* (P) Penguin, London 1978 *The Evacuees* (P) Penguin, London 1978
Trease, Geoffrey	*Red Towers of Granada* (*) Macmillan, London 1966
Wesker, Arnold	*Chicken Soup With Barley* (P) Penguin, London 1964 *Roots* (P) Penguin, London 1964 *I'm Talking About Jerusalem* (P) Penguin, London 1964 *Old Ones* (P) Jonathan Cape, London 1973
Zangwill, Israel	*Children of the Ghetto* White Lion, London 1972 *King of the Schnorrers* H. Pordes, London 1963

For a fully comprehensive bibliography covering all aspects of Anglo-Jewish life, see Ruth Lehmann's *Anglo-Jewish Bibliography* Jewish Historical Society of England, London 1973.

Acknowledgements

Andre Deutsch Fig. 62; BBC Hulton Picture Library Fig. 40; Board of Deputies of British Jews 17.5; Cambridge University Library Fig. 8; Duckworth 24.1; Greater London Council Fig. 41; Jewish Chronicle Fig. 47,66; Keter Publishing Fig. 3,22,26,33,44,64,65; Lincoln City Council Fig. 10; Ordnance Survey Fig. 20; Paul Hamlyn Fig. 63; Penguin Books 4.2; Public Records Office Fig. 2,4,5,7,14,15; Routledge and Kegan Paul 20.4,20.5,20.6,20.7,20.8,20.10, Fig. 50-54; Trustees of the British Museum Fig. 17,29,34; Trustees of the Imperial War Museum, London Fig. 58,59; Vallentine, Mitchell & Co., 24.3; Victoria and Albert Museum Fig. 1; York Minster Fig. 11.